Bibliografische Information der Deutschen Nationalbibliothek

Die Deutsche Nationalbibliothek verzeichnet diese Publikation in der
Deutschen Nationalbibliografie; detaillierte bibliografische Daten sind
im Internet über http://dnb.d-nb.de abrufbar.

ISBN 978-3-8325-3854-5

Logos Verlag Berlin GmbH
Comeniushof, Gubener Str. 47,
10243 Berlin
Tel.: +49 (0)30 42 85 10 90
Fax: +49 (0)30 42 85 10 92
INTERNET: http://www.logos-verlag.de

Understanding and Manipulating Eye Height to Change the User's Experience of Perceived Space in Virtual Reality

Dissertation
der Mathematisch-Naturwissenschaftlichen Fakultät
der Eberhard Karls Universität Tübingen
zur Erlangung des Grades eines
Doktors der Naturwissenschaften
(Dr. rer. nat.)

vorgelegt von:

Markus Leyrer

aus Reutlingen

Tübingen
2014

Tag der mündlichen Qualifikation:	10.10.2014
Dekan:	Prof. Dr. Wolfgang Rosenstiel
1. Berichterstatter:	Prof. Dr. Andreas Schilling
2. Berichterstatter:	Dr. Betty J. Mohler

Abstract

Virtual reality technology can be considered a multi-purpose tool for diverse applications in various domains, e.g. training, prototyping, design, entertainment and research investigating human perception. However, for many of these applications, it is necessary, that the designed, computer-generated virtual environments are perceived from the users as they would be in the real world. Many research studies have shown that this is not necessarily the case. Specifically, egocentric distances are drastically underestimated compared to real world estimates regardless of whether the virtual environment is displayed in a head-mounted display or on an immersive large screen display. While the main reason for this observed distance underestimation is still largely unknown, this dissertation investigates one specific aspect of fundamental importance to distance perception — eye height. In human perception, the ability to determine eye height is essential, because eye height is used to perceive heights of objects, velocity, affordances and distances, all of which allow for successful environmental interaction. It is reasonably well understood that eye height is used to determine many of these percepts. Yet, how eye height itself is determined as well as the process by which eye height is determined across various environmental and physiological changes is still unknown. I used virtual reality and real world experiments to systematically investigate the contributions of visual and body-based information to determine eye height for perceiving distances. The results suggest that if there is a discrepancy between visual and body-based information and no possibility for calibration is provided, humans rely more on their body-based cues for determining their eye height to scale distances and disregard visual information specifying eye height. This has major implications for many virtual reality setups. Based on these findings, I show that because humans rely on their body-based eye height, this can be exploited to systematically alter the perceived space in immersive virtual environments. Thus, eye height manipulations in virtual environments could be a solution to reduce or even counter the usually observed distance underestimation in virtual environments, without many of the drawbacks of alternative approaches to counter distance underestimation in virtual environments. In this dissertation, I demonstrate that eye height can be informed by body-based cues and that this can be exploited to compensate for individual differences in distance compression, which might be sufficient to enable every user an experience close to what was intended by the programmer.

Zusammenfassung

In verschiedensten Bereichen, beispielsweise Training, Prototypenentwicklung, Design, Unterhaltung und Wahrnehmungsforschung, sind virtuelle Realitäten heute ein oft genutztes und vielseitiges Werkzeug. Für viele Anwendungen in diesen Bereichen ist es unabdingbar, die entworfenen und computergenerierten virtuellen Welten als gleichermaßen natürlich wie die reale Welt wahrzunehmen. Allerdings zeigen Studien, dass dies nicht unbedingt der Fall ist. Speziell egozentrische Distanzen werden im Vergleich zu Distanzen in der realen Welt deutlich unterschätzt – unabhängig davon, ob die virtuelle Welt durch eine Datenbrille oder auf einem großen, immersiven Bildschirm dargestellt wird. Während die Ursache für diese Distanzunterschätzung bisher weitgehend unbekannt ist, untersucht die vorliegende Arbeit einen grundlegenden Aspekt für die Wahrnehmung von Entfernungen: die Augenhöhe. Die Fähigkeit, die Augenhöhe zu bestimmen, ist in der menschlichen Wahrnehmung essenziell. Sie dient der Einschätzung von Objekthöhen, Geschwindigkeiten, Distanzen und sogenannten Affordances, welche für eine erfolgreiche Interaktion mit unserer Umwelt erforderlich ist. Wie die Augenhöhe dem Menschen hilft, seine Umgebung zu erfassen, ist relativ gut untersucht. Jedoch ist bisher nicht erforscht, wie die Augenhöhe selbst ermittelt wird und auch der Prozess, mit dem die Augenhöhe in wechselnden Umgebungen und während physiologischer Veränderungen bestimmt wird, ist bisher unbekannt. An diesem Punkt setzt die vorliegende Arbeit an und untersucht durch Experimente in virtueller und realer Welt den jeweiligen Anteil von visuellen und körperbasierten Informationen zur Bestimmung der Augenhöhe. Die Ergebnisse zeigen, dass Menschen sich, wenn eine Diskrepanz zwischen visuellen und körperbasierten Informationen zur Bestimmung der Augenhöhe besteht, eher auf die körperbasierten Wahrnehmungen verlassen. Die visuellen Informationen bleiben weitgehend unbeachtet. Dies hat weitreichende Auswirkungen für neue und bereits existierende Virtual Reality Setups. Die Tatsache, dass Menschen sich vor Allem auf ihre körperbasierte Augenhöhe verlassen, kann ausgenutzt werden, um die Distanzwahrnehmung im virtuellen Raum für den Benutzer systematisch zu verändern. Folglich können Manipulationen der virtuellen Augenhöhe in virtuellen Umgebungen eine Lösung sein, um die für gewöhnlich beobachtete Distanzunterschätzung in virtuellen Welten zu reduzieren oder sogar völlig aufzuheben. Nachteile von alternativen Ansätzen, die ebenfalls versuchen, die Distanzunterschätzung zu verringern, fallen dabei nicht an. Dies könnte bereits ausreichen, um jedem Benutzer die korrekte Wahrnehmung der virtuellen Welt zu ermöglichen, so wie sie vom Programmierer vorgesehen ist.

Acknowledgements

The submission of this dissertation highlights the end of highly interesting, motivating and unique three years of research. These three years provided me with a completely new, stimulating experience of critical thinking, working and dealing with problems, and during these three years, many people contributed to this experience in different ways.

Specifically, I want to thank my supervisors during my time here at the Max Planck Institute for Biological Cybernetics, Dr. Betty Mohler and Dr. Sally Linkenauger for their support, patience, advice and all the many fruitful and often critical discussions about my research. I learned so much from both, all of which helped me to survive in the world of academia and I am grateful to have had both as mentors, who were never tired of providing guidance and a helping hand. Similarly, I want to thank Prof. Heinrich Bülthoff for providing me with the possibility to work in an outstanding research environment, which enabled me to conduct research using state-of-the-art equipment in an open, friendly and international surrounding. Furthermore, I want to thank him, for continuously supporting my research and also providing useful and critical feedback for my work. Also, I would like to thank Prof. Andreas Schilling for co-supervising my work, and all the useful discussions and ideas regarding my research. I am also grateful to all members of my defense committee, Prof. Andreas Schilling, Dr. Betty Mohler, Prof. Alexandra Kirsch and Prof. Heinrich Bülthoff for their time and interest in my research.

I especially want also to thank all my colleagues, who made this last three years during my doctoral studies a very memorable and enjoyable experience. First of all I want to thank all my colleagues at the Max Planck Institute, specifically, Dr. Florian Soyka, Laura Fademrecht, Ivelina Alexandrova, Dr. Ekaterina Volkova, Dr. Trevor Dodds, Dr. Stephan Streuber, Dr. Tobias Meilinger, Dr. Martin Dobricki, Aurelié Saulton and Rainer Boss for creating such an enjoyable working environment with lively and enthusiastic discussions about science and also about my work. Furthermore, I want to express my gratitude for Dr. Harald Teufel and Michael Kerger, for always having a helping hand for preparing experiments and especially Joachim Tesch for the continuous technical support and help with the virtual reality equipment.

I am also very grateful to have had the opportunity to conduct my research within a European Research Project, which allowed me to get invaluable insights into large scale research efforts and to work with fascinating people. Thus, I would like to thank the whole VR-Hyperspace consortium for the amazing experience during the last three years.

Finally, I would like to thank my friends, who always supported and pushed me forward during my adventure of getting my doctoral degree. Furthermore, I would like to thank my family for always trusting in me and supporting me with my goals in life. I want to thank my sisters, Dagmar Bockstaller and Jennifer Leyrer and my parents, Eveline and Ottmar Leyrer for their continuous love and support throughout my life. In addition, I also want to express my gratitude for Ingeborg, Rolf, Julia and Anna Marstaller, as well as Ingeburg Fritz for the overwhelming support during the last years.

Last, but not least, I cannot express how thankful I am for the person, who always supported and loved me during good and bad times on the journey during the last years, Elisabeth Marstaller.

What is real?

How do you define 'real'?

If you're talking about what you can feel,

what you can smell, what you can taste and see,

then 'real' is simply electrical signals

interpreted by your brain.

MORPHEUS TO NEO (THE MATRIX, 1999)

Contents

List of Abbreviations

2D / 3D	Two / Three Dimensions
CAVE	CAVE Automatic Virtual Environment
DFOV	Display Field-of-View
FOV	Field-of-View
GFOV	Geometrical Field-of-View
HMD	Head-mounted Display
IPD	Inter-Pupillary Distance
IVE	Immersive Virtual Environment
LSID	Large Screen Immersive Display
MPI	Max Planck Institute
VE	Virtual Environment
VR	Virtual Reality
VRPN	Virtual Reality Peripheral Network

Chapter 1

Introduction

With the recent progress in virtual reality technology and the increase in computational power, virtual reality is now a very useful tool for a large variety of applications in very diverse domains. The possibility to easily provide users with sophisticated immersive virtual environments (IVEs) delivered via large screen immersive displays (LSIDs) or head-mounted displays (HMDs) has turned virtual reality (VR) into a Swiss army knife for applications ranging from training, prototyping, design, medical rehabilitation and entertainment to research in human perception, scientific visualization and more. However, to be effective, many of these applications require that the displayed virtual environments (VEs) are visually perceived as a replica of the real world (e.g. in design processes) and recent research focusing on human visual perception in IVEs suggests that this is not straight-forward to achieve.

Specifically, egocentric distances, i.e. the distance from a human observer to an object, a main component of the spatial layout of our surrounding environment, is systematically underestimated in IVEs [92, 202, 175, 216, 130, 98, 146] compared to the observed performance in the real world [119, 71, 166], regardless of the measure used. In addition, this underestimation is reported across different laboratories including different systems and as such represents a general problem in the perception of the spatial layout of IVEs (see [160] for a recent review). Thus, the ideal solution to make IVEs more effective would be to discover the reasons for the commonly occurring misperceptions of egocentric distances. However, the reasons for the observed underestimation are still unknown, although some investigators tried to identify the sources to be able to compensate for the existing bias in egocentric distance perception in IVEs. These efforts focused mainly on the investigation of technical aspects of VEs, such as the ergonomics of an HMD [215], restricted field-of-view [92, 34], inaccurate stereo cues [214], distortions introduced by the optics of an HMD [98], calibration issues [98] or the quality of graphics of the VE [202], all of which might influence and bias human perception. However, none of these factors explains the entirety of the occurring underestimation in IVEs. Thus, it is likely that the observed underestimation is a complex problem, which can not be explained by only considering the technical limitations of current IVEs. As a result, two different approaches to solve the underestimation problem in IVEs have emerged: One approach is to provide the users training and feedback within an IVE until the spatial performance is accurate [130, 131, 205, 162]. The

1

other approach aims at modifying visual cues to distance within an IVE to improve the spatial performance [97, 98, 230] towards veridical distance perception.

This dissertation follows the latter approach of modifying cues for perceived distances, with the goal to keep the majority of the available visual cues unaltered. This research focuses on one specific cue in human perception, which is important in the context of egocentric distance perception, especially in the context of VR — the eye height of the user. The first goal of this dissertation is to understand what sensory information is likely used to determine human eye height and to understand the consequences of the used sensory information on the perception of egocentric distances in the real world and in IVEs. This knowledge is necessary for the second goal, namely providing an applied approach using eye height manipulations to enable a close to veridical perception in IVEs, but also to explore the limitations and implications of such an approach for practical applications.

The research presented in this dissertation draws from both, *computer science* and *perceptual psychology*. Thus, the following sections in the introduction of this dissertation will describe both, the necessary background of VR and the necessary background of human perception to understand the interactions of the two fields and how they both are important to the topic investigated in this dissertation.

1.1 Virtual Realities as Multi-Purpose Technology

With the recent advancements in the necessary technology, VR can be considered a multi-purpose tool for a variety of different applications in various domains. However, only recently the computational power has advanced sufficiently to enable renderings in photorealistic quality on common computer systems including real-time interactions within IVEs. Similarly, the display and projection technology advanced further to provide the user with compelling computer-generated environments on either very large scale systems like powerwall and CAVE (Cave Automatic Virtual Environment, see [36, 35]) systems or on a very small scale for wearable displays, used for example in current HMDs. In this section I will briefly define VR and highlight the diversity of applications, where VR technology is currently in use, along with the requirements for VR technology to be effectively used. These requirements represent some aspects of the motivation for the conducted research. While for some applications a veridical spatial perception is not of fundamental importance, it is crucial for others, e.g. for the purpose of ergonomic evaluations or design reviews.

1.1.1 What is Virtual Reality?

In general, VEs can be characterized as computer-simulations of fictional or close to real environments, with which the user can interact. There have been numerous attempts to define VR, however, as Steuer [194] points out, many older definitions are mainly focused on technical aspects as the following attempts of defining VR demonstrate:

"The illusion of participation in a synthetic environment rather than external observation of such an environment. VR relies on a three-dimensional, stereoscopic head-tracker display, hand/body tracking and binaural sound. VR is an immersive, multi-sensory experience." [68]

"Virtual Reality is an alternate world filled with computer-generated images that respond to human movements. These simulated environments are usually visited with the aid of an expensive data suit which features stereophonic video goggles and fiber-optic data gloves." [72]

"The terms virtual worlds, virtual cockpits, and virtual workstations were used to describe specific projects.... In 1989, Jaron Lanier, CEO of VPL, coined the term virtual reality to bring all of the virtual projects under a single rubric. The term therefore typically refers to three-dimensional realities implemented with stereo viewing goggles and reality gloves." [94]

All of those definitions focus on technological aspects of VR, namely the use of *stereo video goggles* and *data* or *reality gloves*. While all VR studies presented in this dissertation are conducted using a HMD, the obtained results should optimally apply also to other VR systems. Thus, throughout this dissertation, VR is considered as:

...a computer interface, which surrounds the user with sensory information (e.g. visual, auditory, etc...) and allows for interaction with a simulated environment. This in turn provides the user with some sort of "presence" and/or "telepresence", both of which refer to the sense of being in the simulated, computer-generated environment.[1]

Furthermore, throughout this dissertation the focus is mainly on the visual experience, although other sensory information can greatly contribute to the feeling of being in the VE. However, some of the most compelling VEs are solely relying on the stimulation of the visual modality (also using body/head-tracking) to generate a feeling of presence for the user. In addition, in the context of this dissertation, the visual system and visual perception within VEs along with information derived from our body is the main focus for the conducted research, therefore other potentially contributing sensory information will not be described.

Terminology

In the area of research, different terms describing virtual realities are used interchangeably and the term VE is often used to describe very different sorts of experiences. Throughout this dissertation I will use the terms VE and IVE with the following distinctions:

VE *The term **virtual environments** applies to all VR experiences, even the simplest form of virtual reality, which is presented using a conventional monitor and displaying a monoscopic image of the virtual scene (Desktop-VR). However, this term also applies to large*

---

[1]For a more detailed discussion about the origin of the term virtual reality see the essay of Steve Bryson [20], also see Steuer [194] and Loomis and colleagues [118] for a discussion about VR and what contributes to VR in different contexts. See also Slater and Wilburs work on immersion and presence [184].

screen projection systems, which can provide stereoscopic viewing and a compelling visual experience and extends to specialized systems and displays. Thus, VE is the overall umbrella term used for every kind of virtual worlds.

IVE *The term **immersive virtual environments** is used in this dissertation to specifically describe virtual worlds, which allow the user to totally immerse her/himself in the computer-generated environment. Within IVEs the scene is usually updated according to the user's position and head movements. Examples for IVEs are mainly HMD based virtual environments, however also CAVEs and other highly specialized displays can completely surround the user and provide tracking of the user and as such lead to a high level of immersion.*

1.1.2 Applications and Requirements

Despite the usually high costs of VR technology and the required expertise, there is already a wide range of current and proposed applications using VEs and many of those applications serve a specific goal and have as such different requirements. While for example many training simulators aim to provide procedural training where veridical spatial accuracy is not necessary, other simulators with the goal of training specific skills like spatial navigation or orienting oneself require an accurate spatial performance. In this section I highlight different areas of applications[2], which may depending on their goals have a reduced effectiveness due to the underestimation of distances in IVEs.

Training and Education

Since Link's invention of the first flight simulator in 1929 [112], a precursor of today's VEs, they are in frequent use to train pilots. First applications are usually reported for military purposes [140]. However, also civil companies make extensive use of flight simulators to train their pilots because of the reduced operating costs and risks in comparison of using real aircrafts [88, 138]. Similarly, training simulators are now commonly used for different types of vehicles, like cars, tanks, helicopters and many others, which allow for a cost-effective and risk free learning of the vehicle or simulations of specific aspects (e.g. behavior of a car in a traffic accident) [141, 120, 25].

Another important field for using VR technology in training and education is the medical domain, albeit many of these applications are non-immersive desktop VEs. Nevertheless, there are numerous simulators for many different areas of surgeries, e.g. for laparoscopic, thoracic, gynaecological, orthopedic, neuro and combat surgery [17, 173, 169, 108, 2, 126]. The trend of using VEs to train medical personal continues, with new applications, also using IVEs, emerging. One current example is training students how to interact with patients using IVEs [5]. Although military scenarios, vehicle simulation and medical scenarios are representing the most common use of VEs in training and education, there are many other applications like training for fire fighters to train how to effectively combat a fire and training personnel how to respond to

---

[2]During the last decades, the number of used and proposed applications using VEs has constantly grown. Thus, I only present a small selection in this dissertation. The references provide more detailed information and provide in part cross-references to further applications.

disasters [7, 79]. While the advantages of using VEs as simulators for training and education are obvious (e.g. risk-free and cost-effective), an accurate spatial perception is crucial for some of those applications to be effective.

Visualization, Design and Evaluation

Another important domain where VR technology is extensively used is the area of visualization, design and corresponding evaluation. For many applications in this domain an accurate spatial perception is not necessary, for example the visualization of proteins, chemical structures and geographical data [19, 28]. Consider the example of visualizing proteins [1]: they can help researchers and students to better understand the structure and composition of different parts, and make it possible to interactively manipulate and explore different components of the visualized protein structure. In this case, an accurate absolute spatial perception is not necessary, because the scale for the visualization is an artificially chosen one with the goal to enable a better exploration, while maintaining the relative size of the corresponding parts.

In contrast, for architectural visualizations or virtual prototyping/assembly, a veridical spatial performance is crucial [44, 180]. For example, the benefit of walking through a virtual architectural model to evaluate it, is very limited if the dimensions of the different structures and rooms are not perceived as they are intended by the designer [76]. Similarly, virtual prototyping requires veridical space perception, for example while evaluating a new virtual prototype of a car model, as has been done for years by the automotive industry [33, 181]. Furthermore, this applies also to all ergonomic evaluations in VEs, although the perceptual limitations are often not fully considered [180, 50].

Teleoperation

An application area, which shares some aspects with the already discussed medical training simulators is teleoperation. The term teleoperation describes the ability to perform a procedure remotely, which can serve different purposes. Besides the medical applications, a prominent example during recent years is the control of unmanned aerial vehicles and (ground-based) robots, either using non-immersive VEs or even IVEs using head mounted displays (see for example [147]), often combined with haptic feedback devices. The advantage of these applications is similar to that of the flight simulators, as it can reduce risks for the human operator, especially in scenarios which can pose danger for the operator, for example for work at disaster sites and work in extreme environments including but not limited to outer space, deep ocean, and nuclear plants (see e.g. [176]).

Entertainment

During the last decades, the entertainment industry has greatly influenced the development of computer graphics and the recent development suggests that this also may apply to the development of VR. Considering the market, it is clear, why the entertainment industry has such an influence. While the market for highly specialized VR equipment is rather small, the market for entertainment includes millions of potential customers. One example for this is the computer gaming industry. Starting out more than three decades ago with simple monochrome games to 16bit VGA games to photorealistic three-dimensional computer graphics in games today, the gaming industry is now a multi-billion dollar industry [47]. Along with the development of graphics for computer games, this market also influences the development of hardware, which is able to render the graphics faster and in a higher resolution, a trend which is for example apparent in the everlasting battle for the fastest gaming graphics card.

In contrast, IVEs have not yet widely been used for gaming and general entertainment purposes. Major factors for this were that IVE technology (e.g. low-latency tracking) used to be very expensive and often required difficult calibration and maintenance. This changed for example with the introduction of the Nintendo Wii in 2006, a console for entertainment purposes, which featured novel wireless interaction methods, which are in part also used within IVEs today and inspired different methods to interact with IVEs [105, 26, 27]. While such gaming consoles are a common entertainment medium nowadays, immersive VR devices are still rare. However, one device, the Oculus Rift has changed this [136]. In contrast to the highly specialized VR technology for specific application areas (e.g. military, medical or specialized training purposes), the Oculus Rift is marketed as a tool for immersive computer games (the founder Palmer Luckey wanted to create a HMD that is usable for computer games). This is also reflected by the price, which is affordable for many households. Thus, the market share provides an incentive to develop this technology further.[3] In addition, the success of the developer prototypes of the Oculus Rift already inspired other companies to announce the development of additional affordable VR technology, i.e. HMDs, interaction devices and more (see for example the newly announced Sony Morpheus HMD or various Kickstarter Projects like the Omni[4]).

Psychology and Psychophysics Research, Therapy and Rehabilitation

One of the most prominent domains for using VEs is the area of research [15, 118, 200], therapy [168, 167, 93] and rehabilitation [104, 172, 78]. VEs are perfectly designed for such applications, as especially in truly immersive VEs it is possible to control all aspects of the environment presented to the user, an aspect, which is important for both, research and therapy. Specifically, it is possible to fully control different stimuli and to investigate (or use) a specific stimulus also in isolation, which might be difficult or even impossible achieve in the real world. In addition, VR technology allows for new experimental paradigms for example in neuroscience, as it provides researchers with the possibility to present *ecologically valid*[5] environments within

---

[3]In personal communication with a staff member of a leading reseller of VR hardware in Germany, he noted that all the specialized HMDs manufactures (e.g. NVIS, Sensics, Emagin and others) do not put much effort in further developing their existing HMDs or developing new models, as the market for this specialized equipment is rather small. Also for industry use, those classic HMDs are still quite expensive and the ergonomics often limited. It is an open question how much influence the announcement of the Oculus Rift on the development of VR technology in the next years will actually have. However, given the fact that Facebook bought Oculus, many VR researchers feel (e.g. Keynote-speech of Henry Fuchs, IEEE VR 2014 in Minneapolis) that there will be a major shift in VR technology, that will have an impact on all related fields.

[4]https://www.kickstarter.com/projects/1944625487/omni-move-naturally-in-your-favorite-game

[5]The term *ecologically valid* refers to experimental conditions and stimuli, which are reasonably well comparable to the setting in the real world [15]. The validity may vary depending on the quality of the sensory cues, i.e. a contextually rich environment can be considered more valid than a environmental setting which is reduced to only the necessary features for an experiment.

an experimental setup, where other configurations are not suitable, e.g. HMDs can be used to display ecologically valid visual stimuli in experiments using brain imaging techniques [15].

During the last decades, many different research areas made extensive use of IVEs to investigate different topics including but not limited to spatial cognition and navigation [59], spatial perception [206], social interaction [42], presence [185] and embodiment [186], multisensory integration [23, 22, 49] and others. For example in the area of spatial navigation, VR technology has proven to be an effective tool to investigate how we navigate through our environment and what representation we use to do so [59]. This is possible by being able to fully control the stimuli and interaction within the VE, a method which is also beneficial for other research areas, e.g. social interaction. There the experimenter can easily control the context in the environment and also record the behavior of the participants in response to a specific stimulus. For example Bailenson, a leading social scientist from Stanford University, uses VEs for social behavior and interaction research. Specifically, he investigates gaze behavior, personal space or interactions between two different virtual selfs (e.g. differing in height, race, gender etc.) [8, 58, 229].

In addition to this brief overview of basic research, several researchers have also demonstrated the effectiveness of using VEs for therapeutic applications, especially in three different areas, namely psychiatric disorder treatment, pain management and neurorehabilitation (see [15] for an extensive review). For example in the area of phobia treatment, VEs provide an easy way, to systematically introduce a feared object or feared situation (e.g. placing the patient with flight anxiety in a virtual airplane) with an appropriate "dose", allowing the therapist to fully control the exposure in a risk-free way [167]. However, VEs do not need to be frightening to be of therapeutical use, the opposite is also true. For rehabilitative therapy, for example for recovering function after a stroke, VEs can be highly engaging and motivating to make it easier for the patients to consistently exercise [78]. In addition, the underlying VR technology often allows the therapist to monitor the achieved improvements of the patients over time [15]. With further developments in the technology it is very likely that the usage of VR technology in the therapeutic field increases.

Summary

This excerpt of current and proposed applications provides an overview of the various domains where VEs are already in use today, which also highlights some of their requirements, for example a veridical spatial performance. As discussed before, research investigating human perception in VEs suggests that spatial performance in VEs is often not comparable to the performance in the real world and the reason is likely a complex interaction between technological issues and human perception. Thus, it is not only sufficient to understand how to generate a VE on a given device, but finally to also understand how humans perceive this VE considering human perception.

1.1.3   State-of-the-Art VR Technology and Current Limitations

Many of the discussed applications rely on state-of-the-art VR technology, which continuously improved during the last decades. Since the first development of an apparatus which could be considered a VE in the year 1929, when Edwin Link patented his first flight simulator [112], VR technology continuously improved. Nevertheless, it took more than 30 years for VEs to appear, which are depicting what is considered a VE today[6]. In 1968 the computer scientist Ivan Sutherland developed the first virtual reality system, which is considered to be the first HMD, already including head tracking for providing a correct stereo view in correspondence to the users' head movements [199].

Since then, VR technology steadily improved and new developments in hardware as well as software, enable computer scientists today to provide the users with compelling imagery and experiences for various applications. In this section I will briefly describe state-of-the-art hardware and software I worked with during my doctoral studies. I will also point out current limitations of this hard- and software, which are also emphasizing the necessity to further investigate how a user perceives the virtual worlds.

VR Hardware

Although the term VR is also used to describe multi-sensory experiences, for example stimulating not only the visual, but also the auditory, olfactory or haptic system, I will focus on hardware to convey the virtual world visually to the user in natural viewing and movement conditions. This has been (and still is) the the most commonly used form of VR and is the main reason for the exciting potential of VR, because one can create worlds with specific characteristics that are fully customizable. Thus, rich and realistic visual details can be included to create a compelling imagery or the visual scene can be artificially impoverished to investigate a specific visual stimulus in isolation. This flexibility and control is not achievable in a real world testing environment. To convey these visual virtual worlds to the user, different types of displays have been used.

Traditionally, common desktop displays were used to visualize the different VEs in combination with a control device (e.g. mouse, joystick) to interact with the environment. Despite the increase in the display quality and resolution, desktop displays are usually non-immersive, have a limited field-of-view (FOV) and do not allow for much natural movement of the user. Other displays, also called large screen immersive displays (LSIDs) like a CAVE [36, 35], powerwalls (see **Figure 1-1**) and semispherical LSIDs, like the PanoLab at the Max Planck Institute (MPI) for Biological Cybernetics in Tübingen, provide the user with a much wider FOV by projecting the VE on walls which surround the participant (see **Figure 1-2**). However, often these displays allow only for a limited range of motions (e.g. for interacting with the VE), which in turn also limits the possibilities for natural interactions.

Apart from the described displays, HMDs are perhaps one of the most widely used VR visualization systems for specific tasks where the user needs to be able to interact with the

---

[6]For the interested reader, I recommend the article from Mazuryk & Gervautz [125], which provides a very detailed description regarding historical technology and applications in VR.

Figure 1-1: The back-projection large screen display consists of a single SXGA+ projector (Christie Mirage S+3K DLP) and a large, flat screen (2.2 meters wide by 2 meters high). The projector has a high contrast ration of 1500:1 and can be used for mono or active stereo projections. In addition, this setup features four Vicon V-series cameras for optical motion-tracking, for example to track the NVIDIA 3DVision Pro active shutter glasses used for the stereo projection setup. Furthermore, a SmartTrack device from ART is available for optical tracking in the space.

Figure 1-2: The Panolab is a half-cylindrical virtual reality projection system, which features a 230° horizontal and 125° vertical FOV and an additional floor projection. The image projection setup consists of 6 Eyevis LED DLP projectors (1920 × 1200 pixels resolution each) and the images are generated by a render cluster consisting of six client image generation PCs and one master PC with frame-synchronized graphics cards to avoid tearing. To compensate for visual distortions due to the curved projection screen, as well as to achieve soft-edge blending for seamless overlap areas, a flexible warping solution using the new warp and blend features of the NVIDIA Quadro chipsets was developed at the Max Planck Institute for Biological Cybernetics. Diverse input devices like the Razer Hydra can be used to interact with the displayed VEs.

VE. Today, HMDs range in size, weight, resolution and the provided FOV. Typically the FOV, weight and ergonomics are the main limitations of HMDs. Nevertheless, HMDs provide a highly immersive experience, because the visual information is usually restricted to that provided by the HMD by blocking out the surrounding environment. The greatest advantage of HMDs is a certain degree of mobility while ensuring a correct sensory-motor coupling, which allows for natural interaction within a VE. In addition, for example in space perception research, many measures require a certain degree of mobility, which is not achievable in the described LSID setups. Thus, for the research presented in this dissertation I relied on HMDs for the conducted experiments, which allowed me to employ different measures and to provide the participants with a more natural interactive experience.

To achieve this, almost all presented experiments in this dissertation were conducted in a free-walking and tracking laboratory in the Cyberneum, which is part of the MPI for Biological Cybernetics. This space a is a large (11.9 m × 11.7 m in size and 8 m high), empty space equipped with 16 high-speed motion capture cameras (Vicon MX 13, see **Figure 1-3**). Using this high-precision motion tracking system, the user can freely explore the virtual world comparable to the experience the user would have in the real world, because the visual rendering of the virtual world is updated according to the movements of the user. This is achieved by capturing for example the head motions of a single or even multiple persons by tracking infra-red reflective markers in real-time. The tracking data is then transmitted wirelessly via the VRPN protocol to either a mobile or stationary graphics system, which updates the VE according to the person's position and generates a correct visualization of the virtual world. The participants can navigate freely in this tracking space if desired by either using a wireless video transmission setup or by using a backpack carrying the video unit of the corresponding HMD and a visualization system, which is usually carried by the experimenter. To enhance the experience of the virtual world, the laboratory is completely dark with the possibility to block out all light and has acoustic panels on the walls to reduce reverberations.

For visually conveying the VE to the participants, I could chose between four state-of-the-art HMDs, all with advantages and disadvantages, namely the Kaiser SR80 ProView, the nVisor SX60, the nVisor SX111 or the Oculus Rift DK1. The Kaiser SR80 ProView has a FOV of 63° horizontally and 53° vertically, a resolution 1280 × 1024 pixels and weighs 790 grams. The Kaiser SR80 has a good resolution and FOV, a contrast of 100:1, is rather lightweight and features stereo with 100% overlap. However, the Kaiser SR80 is not powered by a battery, which limits its use in scenarios where the user has to walk or interact with the VE (see **Figure 1-4**). Furthermore, due to the ergonomics of the HMD, the surrounding environment is not completely blocked out, which can have undesired side effects, depending on the experimental question.

The nVisor SX60 is one of the most common used HMDs in the area of space perception research in the VR research community. The nVisor SX60 has a FOV of 44° horizontally and 35° vertically, a resolution of 1280 × 1024 pixels per eye, a refresh rate of 60 Hz per eye and a contrast of 100:1. However, this HMD is relatively heavy, weighing 1.7 kilograms including the attached markers for tracking the head movements of the participant (see **Figure 1-5**). Nevertheless, the nVisor SX60 has a nice image quality and with the attached felt blocks out the

Figure 1-3: The Tracking Lab is an empty free-walking space with a 16-camera optical tracking system (Vicon MX13). The space is fully tracked, which allows the person to explore virtual environments in a natural way with congruent body-based and visual information.

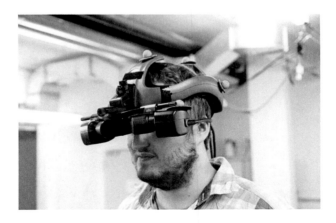

Figure 1-4: A participant wearing the Kaiser SR80 ProView HMD.

surrounding environment. In addition, the SX60 can be used with batteries, which makes the system mobile because all related necessary equipment (e.g. laptop, video signal splitter etc.) can be carried on a backpack. Similarly, the nVisor SX111 (see **Figure 1-6**) has comparable specifications, but a large FOV of approximately 102° horizontally and 64° vertically, with the same resolution, refresh rate and contrast compared to the nVisor SX60. However, to achieve the large horizontal FOV the SX111 has only 66% overlap for the images of the two eyes. While the visual image quality in the SX111 is very good, it suffers from a severe limitation: due to the optics the HMD weighs over 2 kilograms. Thus, this HMD is only usable for very short (<30 minutes) experiments where the participant ideally does not need to move much or is seated.

Figure 1-5: A participant wearing the nVisor SX60 HMD including attached markers for optical position tracking.

Figure 1-6: A participant wearing the nVisor SX111 HMD including attached markers for optical position tracking.

Finally, in 2012 the Oculus Rift was announced, a low budget HMD with a built-in head (orientation only) tracker and a wide field-of-view marketed for the computer game industry, which is already available as a developer kit with a reduced resolution. While the Oculus Rift is a very promising HMD, the reduced resolution of only 640 × 800 pixels per eye is a current limitation. Nevertheless, the Oculus Rift DK1 has a FOV of 106° horizontally and weighs only 380 grams combined with an ergonomic design, which can be compared to ski goggles (see **Figure 1-7**). Thus, the Oculus Rift is very lightweight and easy to wear, also for prolonged durations, even with a completely wireless lightweight setup. However, as the Oculus Rift is rather new, there is no empirical research yet how virtual worlds are perceived or about the introduced distortions due to the HMD itself. Nevertheless, the Oculus Rift is a very promising display device for future research.

Figure 1-7: A participant wearing the Oculus Rift DK1 including attached markers for optical position tracking.

In summary, all described HMDs provide certain advantages, but have also some limitations. Because of the fact that the nVisor SX60 is one of the HMDs, which is in use in different laboratories around the world, the possibility for mobile setups and the well documented performance in perceptual tasks with this display, I chose to conduct the studies presented in this dissertation with the nVisor SX60.

VR Software

Virtual worlds need to be programmed before they can be displayed in different VR setups, and there are many software solutions and engines, which aid the programmer in creating compelling VEs. For creating VEs I used several different software solutions. For some of the conducted experiments I used Virtools 5 from Dassault Systèmes, which is easy to use for programming experiments and sharing solutions with other scientists. Through a graphical programming interface, Virtools enabled also non-programmers to develop their own experiments and for advanced programmers, Virtools offered a scripting language (see **Figure 1-8**). However, Virtools was marketed (is now discontinued) as an authoring tool, and the graphical quality of the rendering was rather limited.

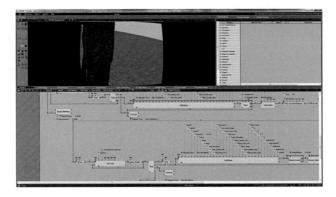

Figure 1-8: The editor of Virtools 5 used for programming virtual environments using a graphical programming interface.

Thus, I switched to Unity 3D[7], which is a game development platform and also available for free, if no "pro-features" are needed. It combines a powerful rendering engine, which is fully integrated with an editor to create interactive 3D and 2D content. The graphical quality is state-of-the-art and Unity is widely used in the entertainment industry to create games for diverse platforms (see **Figure 1-9**). Unity 3D allows for programming in multiple languages (e.g. C#, Javascript, Boo, Lua) and because of the widespread use, a wide selection of third party tools is available. In addition, I use MiddleVR (from I'm in VR) as a middleware, which makes it easy to use all the described VR equipment in a VE programmed with Unity3D. With MiddleVR it is easy to use an experiment in different HMDs setups with different specifications or to even display the VE on a LSID or desktop display, without the need to change the code of the VE.

Finally, a promising alternative to Unity 3D is the Unreal Engine 4[8] (see **Figure 1-10**). The advantage of Unreal Engine 4 is the superior graphics quality compared to Unity 3D and the recently announced licensing model, which makes it an attractive alternative to Unity 3D. In the Unreal Engine 4, programming is in C++ using Microsoft Visual Studio or Apple's Xcode developer. In addition, as a subscriber one gets full source code access of the engine. With the fully integrated support of the Oculus Rift in both engines, Unreal Engine 4 and Unity 3D, they seem like promising candidates for the development of future VR applications and experiments.

---

[7]http://unity3d.com/unity
[8]https://www.unrealengine.com/

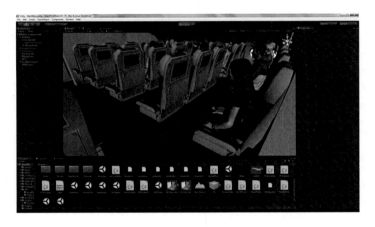

Figure 1-9: The editor of Unity 3D. For programming, either the provided Mono-Studio or other development tools like Microsoft Visual Studio can be used with Unity3D.

Figure 1-10: The editor of the Unreal Engine 4. For programming Visual Studio from Microsoft is used.

Current Limitations

Despite the recent improvements in VR technology, there are still some limitations, also for state-of-the-art VR technology. For example, setups like the described semi-spherical screen (the Panolab) require warped images due to curved projection surfaces. Because a calibration of such spaces is often computationally expensive or for reasons of simplicity, the warping is often only calculated for a predefined viewpoint, i.e. a defined position on the floor and an eye height of for example 1.70 meters. This means, that participants either larger or smaller than this predefined viewpoint might perceive the VE differently compared to participants with an eye height of approximately 1.70 meters. Thus, it is important to investigate what perceptual consequences for example a difference between the actual and visual eye height has on perception. Comparable issues apply for all VR setups, where no head tracking is available. Similarly, for many setups, which can be used for multiple users (e.g. imagine a collaborative task in a CAVE), often only one person has a correct visual perspective of the VE. Thus, the other users will likely perceive a different image of the virtual space, than the user with the correct perspective, which likely hinders successful collaboration on a given task (there are a few exceptions with setups which provide a correct stereo view for multiple users). The most compelling setup addressing this specific problem is the multi-user powerwall of the VR laboratory of Bernd Fröhlich at the Bauhaus Universität Weimar [99]. With a sophisticated setup, they manage to provide up to six users with a correct image in stereo, which circumvents the issue that every user has a different view on the virtual world. Hence, while some of the current issues can be solved with an increase in computational power and network capacities (i.e. fast calculation and rendering of different warpings and different perspectives in sufficient quality), there are other issues, which likely include issues with the perception of IVEs. Even for HMDs, where the technical issues (e.g. FOV, weight, resolution etc.) can be likely be solved with further development, these technical issues (which will be discussed in detail in section 2.2.2) do not explain the entirety of one major limitation, which applies to all state-of-the-art setups: The VEs are often not perceived as intended by the programmer. Regardless of whether a HMD, LSID or powerwall is used, egocentric distance, which is a main component of the spatial layout of an environment, is drastically underestimated throughout various setups using different VR technology with different specifications (regarding weight, FOV, resolution and more, e.g. see [146, 148, 90, 34, 92, 202, 213]). This suggests, that because technical factors seem not to explain the entirety of this effect, this underestimation might be the result of a complex interaction between technological issues and human perception. Therefore, it is necessary to understand human perception to be able to improve the utility of VEs, despite the advances in VR technology.

1.2   Understanding Human Perception

To understand how humans perceive different VEs on different devices, it is necessary to have a closer look at the process of human perception. Perception is one of the oldest fields within psychology and many different theories about how our perception works have been proposed and discussed during the last centuries. Even before the development of experimental psychology as a modern academic discipline in the early 19th century, human perception was discussed in the context of *epistemology*[9] by many well known philosophers, including but not limited to Descartes, Hume, Locke, Kant and others. Since human perception is so complex, there are still aspects of human perception which are not fully understood and even today there are different theories highly debated (for example see the discussion between Proffitt and Loomis [156, 80, 157, 81], or the recent debate between Proffitt and Firestone [54, 153]), although the knowledge about the functionality of the perceptual system increased considerably. Nevertheless, our perceptual system keeps us alive most of the time, but how?

1.2.1   What is Perception?

The main purposes of perception are to inform us about our surrounding environment to help us to perform different actions within our environment [67]. For doing this, our perceptual system follows a process of sensing or acquiring information, interpret this information and selecting and organizing it for the purpose of understanding what is being sensed and what actions we can perform in the given environment [70]. Specifically, in the common view today, this process consists of 8 steps, which are depicted in **Figure 1-11**. The perceptual process is depicted as a circle (i.e. a closed-loop system), because usually the perceptual process is dynamic and continually changing due to our interaction with the environment [70]. For example acting in the environment changes the perceived environmental stimulus and thus, new information will be acquired which is then processed by the perceptual system and will likely lead to a different action.

Thus, the overall goal of perceptual research is to understand the different steps in the process of perception, which require different levels of analysis. Adapting Goldsteins analogy of a car in traffic, there are possibilities for different levels of analysis [70]. One could observe the traffic and how it is influenced by streets and other cars. One level further we could analyze a single car and investigate its behavior or we could even go deeper and investigate the engine of the car and its single parts. Similar to this analogy there are different levels of analysis for investigating human perception. Throughout this dissertation, I will focus on the so-called *psychophysical*[10] *level of analysis*, which focuses on the relationship of a given stimulus and a person's perception, which is indicated by arrow A in Figure 1-11. While this relationship applies to stimuli acquired

---

[9]Epistemology is one branch of philosophy, of which the focus is on the scope and nature of knowledge, thus also often referred to as the *theory of knowledge*. As a central part of this philosophical branch, perception is the foundation of our empirically gathered "knowledge".

[10]The term psychophysics was introduced in 1860 by Gustav Fechner [51, 52], and usually refers to quantitative methods for measuring relationships between the stimulus and perception, namely measuring the detection thresholds of a given stimuli, e.g. what is the minimally required stimulus intensity that it can be detected. However, as pointed out by Goldstein there are now numerous methods to measure this relationship, why the term psychophysics refers here to the broader context of measuring the stimulus-perception relationship [70].

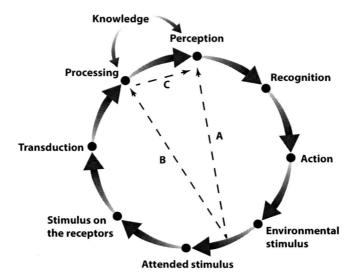

Figure 1-11: The perceptual process model from Goldstein including important relationships: **A:** Stimulus-Perception Relationship; **B:** Stimulus-Physiology Relationship; **C:** Physiology-Perception Relationship. Adapted from [70]

through all our different senses (e.g. visual, auditory or haptic stimuli) I will focus in the context of the presented research on the relationship between visual stimuli (e.g. a given target in the environment) and a corresponding percept (e.g. the target is 5m away from me).

1.2.2   The Difficulty of Measuring Human Perception

Because of the complexity and cognitive nature of human perception, it is difficult to *directly* measure (visual) perception. However, it is possible to *indirectly* measure perception by using measures involving cognitive and motor responses to given controlled stimuli. Depending on the response to a given stimulus, it is possible to infer what the specific perception of the observer of this specific stimulus may be. However, careful consideration is required in choosing the appropriate measure for the given research question. Thus, for the research presented in this dissertation, I will rely on established indirect measures for assessing egocentric distance perception in virtual environments and also in the real world. Furthermore, I will use both, cognitive and motor responses, namely verbal reports and blind walking. Both measures have a long history within the field of space perception, and are commonly used to measure perceived egocentric distances [34, 71, 92, 215, 119, 114, 101, 98, 230][11].

---

[11]During the last decades other measures for assessing egocentric distance perception have been developed, all with advantages and disadvantages, see [160] for a recent overview of different studies using different measures. Some of these measures will be presented and discussed in Section 2.1.3

1.2.3 Human Perception in the Context of Virtual Reality

Human perception in the context of virtual reality can be considered from two perspectives. One perspective is to use virtual reality technology as a tool to investigate human perception [118, 200]. With the amount of control over a visual stimulus offered by VEs, they provide unmatched possibilities for investigating perception by enabling researchers to maintain the exact same ecologically valid visual stimulus across different participants. In addition, using VEs to investigate visual perception enables researchers to separate naturally coincident information (e.g. visual and proprioceptive[12] information [206, 23, 22]), which would be very difficult or not possible to achieve in the real world in an ecologically valid way.

The other perspective is concerned with the perceptual performance within VEs. As highlighted in Section 1.1.2, for the effectiveness of many applications a performance comparable to that in the real world is crucial. However, this is not necessarily the case: Specifically, egocentric distances are commonly underestimated by 20% to 50% compared to real world performance, as has been shown by research investigating human perception in VEs [202, 34, 175, 101, 114]. Consequently, researchers have tried to find the reason for this phenomenon by investigating how VEs are perceived across different setups and systems. While technical limitations or calibration issues seem not to fully explain the observed underestimation (e.g.[97, 98, 215, 214]), it is likely that the underestimation is the result of a complex interaction between technological issues and human perception, which makes it important to further investigate visual perception in VEs and how different cues influence a person's percept of a VE.

1.3 The Role of Eye Height in the Real World and Virtual Reality

One cue for visual perception is eye height, which can be defined as the perpendicular distance from the observers' eyes to the ground plane. Eye height and eye level are closely related to each other and in the literature both terms are sometimes used interchangeably, although eye height is different to the concept of eye level, which could be considered mutable and more akin to line of sight (see **Figure 1-12**).

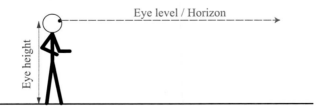

Figure 1-12: The difference between eye height and eye level. **Note:** The eye level is usually coincident with the horizon.

---

[12]Proprioception is the sense for the positioning of our body joints and our body itself. The brain uses the information from the proprioceptive and vestibular system for the overall sense of body position and body motion (e.g. acceleration and velocity).

In studies conducted in the real world, eye height has been identified as an important source of information for perceiving affordances[13] [209, 123], determining velocity [107] and obtaining object height in the visual field [224, 225]. In addition, empirical evidence has supported the notion that eye height is fundamental for perceiving distances [178, 179, 137]. Therefore, eye height plays an important role in perception throughout our everyday life. Consider a small example to illustrate how eye height can influence our perception: revisiting your childhood playground as an adult. Things may seem smaller than you remember them. One possible explanation for such a phenomenon is that humans use their eye height as a metric to scale sizes and distances, and your eye height is much larger as an adult, so the playground appears smaller because it measures a smaller portion of your eye height [153].

However, in the context of virtual reality, the role of eye height is less clear. While some of the previously discussed research concerning eye height has been replicated in VR, for example that eye height is used to perceive object height and affordances [189], other aspects like the influence of eye height or the effects of an inaccurate eye height calibration on perceived distance have received much less attention throughout the literature. In fact, many VR systems do not calibrate eye height properly and use an average eye height for all users. In general, eye height within VEs is an often overlooked factor, and the consequences of this are not really well understood. In addition, the information specifying eye height has not been thoroughly investigated in the real world, which may, depending on the source of information used, have different consequences for the perception within VEs applying to many different applications in various fields.

1.4   Organization of this Dissertation

The research presented in this dissertation has multiple goals: The first goal is to investigate what sensory information is used to specify eye height and the role of body posture in determining eye height. Based on the used sensory information, this may have different consequences on perception in the real world and specifically in VEs. The results and gained understanding from the first part are a requirement for the second goal, which is to provide an applied approach using eye height manipulations to enable a close to veridical perception in IVEs. In addition, one goal is also to explore the limitations and implications of this approach for practical applications. Furthermore, the presented research can be used to derive some guidelines for how eye height should be considered across different VR setups.

To achieve these goals, this dissertation draws from both, the field of computer science and that of perceptual psychology. While VEs have been created and developed within the field of computer science, the research presented in this thesis uses methods and techniques from perceptual psychology to understand the role of human perception in VEs. This knowledge can in turn be used to improve VEs. The advantage of the interdisciplinary approach is, that some of the present problems persisting in VEs, which are affecting a large number of applications in

---

[13]The term affordance was introduced by the psychologist J.J. Gibson in 1977. An affordance is an inherent property of an object or environment, which allows individuals to perform an action [66, 67]. For example a door affords passing through, while a chair has according to Gibson the inherent affordance of sitting on it.

various domains, might only be solvable with a basic understanding of human perception. Thus, the remainder of this dissertation tries to combine both fields.

Specifically, Chapter 2, discusses related research concerning both, the necessary perceptual theory and the related research of space and specifically distance perception within real and virtual environments. Chapter 3 describes the motivation for the presented research and the perceptual theory in the context of computer science (applied) and perceptual psychology (theoretical). Chapter 4 describes the first set of experiments aimed at identifying the sensory information used to specify eye height, and whether this sensory information is updated across different postures within IVEs. Furthermore, two real world experiments are presented, which aim at validating the previously obtained results in the real world, to ensure the generalisability of the presented findings. Chapter 5 describes another set of experiments integrating the findings of the previously conducted experiments with the goal to enable a close to veridical perception in IVEs for an individual user of a VE and Chapter 6 includes a general discussion and summary of the presented results along with a discussion of further questions and potential future work. Finally, Chapter 7 discusses and explores the implications from both a theoretical and practical perspective.

1.4.1 Contributions of the Candidate

The research presented in this dissertation makes several new contributions to both fields, computer science and psychology. Specifically, this research demonstrates cases where humans rely on their body-based senses to scale distances from the body, while many have speculated that humans rely on visual information to determine their eye height. Both the visual and proprioceptive/vestibular (hereafter referred to as "body-based") modalities might provide robust information about eye height. However, because these two modalities naturally co-vary with each other following any possible change in eye height encountered in the real world, it is not trivial to separate these two sources of information to ascertain which source of information (visual or body-based) informs distance perception. Using virtual reality to achieve a conflict in visually and body-based specified eye height revealed a reliance on body-based cues over vision-based eye height information. Thus, this research provides an answer to a basic question in human perception that has been discussed already decades ago and has been described as potentially "untestable". In addition, the prevailing view in the field of visual perception is that visual percepts are determined predominantly by visual information [158]. The presented studies clearly show that basic percepts, such as distances, can be determined by a combination of visual and body-based information. In addition, the findings presented in this dissertation may help to explain some of the perceptual phenomena where our perceptual system fails at providing us with an appropriate feedback of the spatial layout of our environment, for instance when standing at elevated ground surfaces [182].

Most importantly, these findings have major implications for human perception within VEs. In the presented research I demonstrate that because of the previously discussed results a simple eye height manipulation can drastically alter the perceived space in IVEs and as such can be used to reduce (or in many cases even counter) the commonly occurring underestimation of distances, which may be useful for many applications. Thus, I believe that this work will be appealing and important for a wide audience working with virtual reality. In contrast to other attempts to counter distance underestimation in IVEs, the applied eye height manipulation maintains more of the perceptual fidelity of visual aspects of the IVE, because it works with less drastic effects on many visual cues present in a virtual environment. Consequently, this research has several implications for egocentric distance perception in HMD-based IVEs. First of all, the current work emphasizes the importance of a correct calibration of the HMD regarding eye height. Any miscalibration regarding the virtual eye height will likely have effects on the perceived spatial layout of the environment. Specifically, for setups where no accurate head tracking can be provided (e.g. some LSIDs), it is important to measure the physical eye height of the observer and to adjust the virtual camera accordingly to provide comparable conditions for all participants of a different height. However, if this is not possible, with the theoretical framework provided in this dissertation, it is possible to quantify the effect that a discrepancy between virtual and real eye height might have on perceived distances for each individual user.

Finally, the presented research has important practical implications by contributing to previous work trying to counter distance underestimation in IVEs, which is important for several applications that rely on spatial perception mirroring that in the real world. In comparison to previous work, the research in this dissertation shows that manipulating the virtual eye height can be a solution with comparable effects on perceived distances, but with consistent effects across different measures. In addition, the used approach using manipulated eye height is easy to implement and can be applied on an individual basis regardless of the prior misperception present (e.g. over- or underestimation). Thus, the presented approach might be usable in practical scenarios, for example in design reviews, and the eye height manipulation can be based on individual performance to enable every user an experience close to what was intended by the content designer.

The ideas and results of the presented experiments in this dissertation, are in part presented in the following publications:

Leyrer, M., Linkenauger, S.A., Bülthoff, H.H., and Mohler, B. (in revision). **Eye height for perceiving egocentric distances can be determined by non-visual, body-based cues.**

Leyrer, M., Linkenauger, S.A., Bülthoff, H.H., and Mohler, B. (in press). **Eye height manipulations: A possible solution to reduce underestimation of egocentric distances in head-mounted displays.** *ACM Transactions on Applied Perception.*

Leyrer, M., Linkenauger, S.A., Bülthoff, H.H., Kloos U., and Mohler, B. (2011). **The influence of eye height and avatars on egocentric distance estimates in immersive virtual environments.** *In Proceedings of the ACM SIGGRAPH Symposium on Applied Perception in Graphics and Visualization.*

For all presented studies in this dissertation, the ideas were proposed by the candidate. Design, stimulus generation, experimental work and analysis of all results have been predominantly carried out by the candidate. The co-authors role for conducting the presented research was that of supervision, giving advice and offering criticism as well as revising the listed manuscripts. Parts of this dissertation use portions of the listed manuscripts, specifically for the sections describing the conducted empirical work (Chapter 5 and 6).

Not included in this dissertation, but research related to the topic investigated in this dissertation and where I was involved in, can be found in the following publications:

Linkenauger, S.A., **Leyrer, M.**, Bülthoff, H.H., and Mohler, B. (2013). **Welcome to Wonderland: The Influence of the Size and Shape of a Virtual Hand On the Perceived Size and Shape of Virtual Objects.** *PLOS ONE 8(7) 1-16.*

D'Cruz M., Patel H., Lewis L., Cobb S., Bues M., Stefani O., Grobler T., Helin K., Viitaniemi J., Aromaa S., Frohlich B., Beck S., Kunert A., Kulik A., Karaseitanidis I., Psonis P., Frangakis N., Slater M., Bergstrom I., Kilteni K., Kokkinara E., Mohler B.J., **Leyrer M.**, Soyka F., Gaia E., Tedone D., Olbert M. und Cappitelli M. (2014). **Demonstration: VR-HYPERSPACE — The innovative use of virtual reality to increase comfort by changing the perception of self and space** *IEEE Virtual Reality (VR 2014), IEEE, Piscataway, NJ, USA, 167-168*

Leyrer, M., Linkenauger, S.A., Bülthoff, H.H., Kloos U. and Mohler, B. (2011). **Perception of the size of self and the surrounding visual world in immersive virtual environments.** *34th European Conference on Visual Perception, Toulouse, France. Perception, 40(ECVP Abstract Supplement) 209*

Leyrer, M., Linkenauger, S.A., Bülthoff, H.H., Kloos U., and Mohler, B. (2011). **The influence of a scaled third-person animated avatar on perception and action in virtual environments** *11th Annual Meeting of the Vision Sciences Society (VSS 2011), Naples, FL, USA. Journal of Vision, 11(11), 69.*

Chapter 2

Perceiving Distance in Real and Virtual Environments

To be able to improve distance perception in IVEs, it is necessary to understand how humans perceive distances in the real and virtual worlds. Therefore, I borrow knowledge and insight from the field of psychology. In fact, many of the oldest yet still prominent questions in psychology deal with perception — how do humans perceive the world. Specifically, the problem of how humans perceive depth is one of the most basic of these questions: How do we perceive a 3-dimensional environment when the image on the retina of our eye (referred to as *retinal image*), the stimulus for perception, is flat and two-dimensional [151][14]?

In this chapter, I summarize the basics of human distance perception, namely, the specific depth cues that are considered important for disambiguating distances. Given that most consider the stimulus for visual perception to be the two-dimensional image on the back of the retina, it is remarkable that humans are still able to be fairly accurate in perceiving distances [116]. Furthermore, I discuss the problem of measuring the perceived distance: as it is not possible to measure any percept directly, different researchers have developed many methods to indirectly measure the perceived distance.

After introducing the necessary background of human distance perception[15], I will present research closely related to the topic presented in this dissertation, namely distance perception in virtual worlds and the corresponding problem of the underestimation of distances in VEs. I will discuss research investigating the origin of the observed underestimation and also research trying to counter this underestimation with different approaches. Finally, I present how eye height is related to space and specifically distance perception, and why eye height might be an important factor to consider in VEs and may even be used to reduce or counter the observed distance underestimation in VEs.

---

[14]While distances can be ego- (between me and an external object) and exocentric (between two external objects) in nature, the research presented in this dissertation focuses entirely on egocentric distance perception, and when I refer to distance perception I mean egocentric distances if not specified otherwise.

[15]The area of perception is one of the main fields in psychology with a huge body of literature and many different theories. For the reader especially interested in visual perception, I recommend the chapter from Kubovy and colleagues [95], describing the foundations of visual perception, also in the context of different contemporary theories how visual perception is assumed to work in detail, which are beyond the scope of this dissertation.

2.1 The Basics of Human Distance Perception

One of the main components of the spatial layout of our surrounding environment is the ego-centric distance between the observer and any object in the space. This can be the distance to objects which are close to your nose, across the room, down the hallway or even as far as the horizon [70]. However, how do humans perceive distances? According to Proffitt & Caudek, this is one of the paradoxes in understanding perception, because on the one hand it seems there is simply not sufficient information available to perform this task, on the other hand it seems that there is a wealth of information [154]. Thus, in the following sections, I will describe, why one could say that there is not enough information to perceive distances and why there is actually a wealth of information available which enables us to perceive distances.

2.1.1 The Nature of the Information Specifying Depth

To understand the apparent difficulty in perceiving depth, one needs to consider the visual information available to specify distance. In principle, what we perceive from our surrounding environment is not more than light reflected from any point in the surrounding space, which reaches our eye through the pupil and is bent through the cornea and lens in our eye, resulting in an upside-down, two-dimensional image on our retina [160]. Thus, if we only consider a single point, it is impossible to tell, whether the light was reflected from a point a meter away or from a point at a great distance [70]. This fact has already been noted by Berkeley in 1709, where he states that the available information is very limited for perceiving depth. He argues that a point in the environment projects onto the retina in a way which does not vary when the distance to this point changes, why he concluded that the perception of distance from sight alone was impossible [11, 154]. Further, he concluded that supplementary non-visual information is necessary. For example, both eyes need to converge to a given point, thus, proprioceptive information about the position of the eyes can support vision to perceive depth in that closer objects require a higher degree of eye rotation [11]. While Berkeley's assumptions are true for any points in the environment when viewed in isolation, where it indeed would be hard to perceive distance from vision alone, this is not the case in a natural environment and under natural viewing conditions.

When the complexity of our visual environment increases, the information specifying the environment also increases. Consider the example of the one point viewed in isolation, if we add a second point at a different depth, both points will project to different locations on the retina, which already provides information about the relative distance of the points to each other [70, 154]. If we expand this view to the entire image of the surrounding environment, even more information is available, which is used to reconstruct depth from the two-dimensional image projected on the back of the retina. This information is usually described as *cues to depth or distance* and the approach different researchers have taken to explain the information used to derive a three-dimensional image of the two-dimensional image is commonly called the **cue approach** [70]. Due to this research, a large variety of depth cues and their effectiveness across different ranges have been identified (e.g. spatial relations of different objects and other regularities in our environment), which enable the human to perceive depth [38, 37].

2.1.2 Sensory and Depth Cues for Perceiving Space

According to Cutting & Vishton, different lists describing the depth cues used for perceiving the surrounding environment and objects have been around for decades (e.g. [24, 223, 65]), which usually include a selection of different cues, for example "accommodation, aerial perspective, binocular disparity, convergence, height in the visual field, motion perspective, occlusion, relative size, relative density, and often many more" [38]. In this dissertation I will focus on the work of Cutting & Vishton [38], which not only provides an overview of important depth cues but also a comprehensive overview of the effectiveness of different depth cues with increasing distance from the observer.

In principle, depth cues can be divided in two groups: 1. *pictorial depth cues*, which can provide information about depth in a two-dimensional image (i.e. a picture or photograph, or the two-dimensional image on the back of the retina) when seen with only one eye and 2. *non-pictorial depth cues*, which describe information derived from either motion, proprioception (i.e. the oculomotor cues) or the fact that humans have two eyes. A commonality between both groups is that some depth cues have a specific or limited range of effectiveness given a certain viewing distance, which Cutting & Vishton divide into three areas: 1. The *Personal Space*, which describes the area directly around the observer up to approx. 2 meters distance; 2. the *Action Space*, which is used to describe a space usually used for performing actions, i.e. from approx. 2 up to 30 meters and 3. the *Vista Space*, which describes everything beyond approximately 30 meters distance form the observer.

Cutting & Vishton list five pictorial depth cues, namely occlusion, relative size, relative density, height in the visual field, and aerial perspective[16]:

Occlusion: Occlusion occurs when one object is hidden from the perceiver's view by another object. Thus, occlusion only provides information about depth order, as the occluded object must be farther away than the object in front. However, occlusion is only informative for relative distance, it is not possible to perceive absolute distance based on occlusion. Nevertheless, the effective range of occlusion is very impressive and in principle only limited by our visual system's acuity [38].

Relative Size & Relative Density: Relative size describes the relationship between perceived size and distance. Objects that are farther away project smaller images on to the back of our retina. Hence, if it is known that two objects are the same size, then an object that projects a smaller retinal image is farther away. Relative size can also be used to perceive absolute distance information if the size of the object is known (also known as the size-distance hypothesis, see [89, 48] for discussions) and this cue can be used over the whole range of perceivable distances. Related to relative size is relative density if a consistent actual density can be assumed, as clustered objects have a higher density in the retinal image when they are farther away. Both depth cues in combination also explain the usefulness of ground texture information for perceiving distances, a fact which was

---

[16] A very detailed description of these cues, how they can be measured and about their effective ranges can be found in the comprehensive work of Cutting & Vishton [38].

already noted by Gibson in 1950 [65]. It was also recently demonstrated that a textured ground information is helpful for informing distance perception (e.g. see [182, 74, 227]).

Height in the Visual Field: The depth cue height in the visual field (also known as relative height), describes a depth cue which yields good ordinal information about distance. Specifically, objects with bases that are higher in the visual field (or image) are usually seen as further away, assuming they have physical contact to the ground, thus the bases of the objects are located below the horizon, see [70, 38]. However, notice that the opposite occurs for example for clouds - the closer the base of the clouds are seen in relation to the horizon the farther away they are perceived and clouds with the bases on the top of the visual field are usually perceived as closest. Thus, objects which are above the horizon look closer if their bases are higher in the visual field.

Furthermore, Cutting & Vishton [38] also suggest that relative height may yield absolute distance information if a couple assumptions are met: (1) the ground plane must be opaque; (2) gravity is present and it is assumed that every object has physical contact to the supporting surface, e.g. the ground (i.e. the object is not floating); (3) that the observer's eye hight is known (e.g. 1.65 meters above the ground) and (4) that the ground surface is planar and orthogonal to gravity. If these assumptions are met, relative height can yield absolute distance information. However, Cutting & Vishton [38] conclude that "the assumptions which must be made for such information, however, may in many situations be unacceptably strong"[17].

Aerial Perspective: The concept of the depth cue aerial perspective (also called atmospheric perspective) is rather simple: By looking through air, which usually contains small particles like dust and various amounts of moisture or pollution particles, objects in the further distance become less sharp and clear. Also they may become more "blue" and the contrast of the objects can change, see [38, 70]. Aerial perspective is unique amongst the discussed depth cues, as it is the only one where the effectiveness increases with increasing distance up to a certain limit, where objects become indistinguishable [38] and it is also dependent on the atmospheric conditions like weather.

These five cues complete the list of pictorial depth cues, although there are various other candidates listed in the literature, for example texture gradient, linear perspective, brightness, light and shading, kinetic depth, kinetic occlusion and disocclusion, and gravity. However, as pointed out by Cutting & Vishton [38], those cues can be considered either as a combination of the discussed pictorial depth cues (as highlighted for example for relative size and relative density, which explain the effectiveness of texture gradient) or likely do not have a strong influence on the perception of spatial layout[18].

---

[17]In fact, the relationship described by Cutting & Vishton [38] describes the angle of declination below the horizon hypothesis to perceive absolute distance, see [178, 137, 62]. This dissertation is building up on this relationship, which will be described and discussed in detail in section 2.3.2

[18]For an exhaustive list of depth cues including many illustrated examples I recommend the interested reader the excellent book of William B. Thompson and colleagues [201] or the chapter about depth perception from Proffitt & Caudek [154].

However, pictorial depth cues are not the only effective cues for perceiving depth, because the second group of non-pictorial depth cues are additional effective sources of information for perceiving depth in our surrounding environment. Non-pictorial cues are special because they either depend on motion of the observer, or are derived from the anatomy and physiology of the human eyes. Specifically, these cues provide information about distance from motion (motion parallax or motion perspective), the oculomotor system, as already noted by Berkeley in 1709 [11] (accommodation and convergence), and binocular disparity (the fact that an object creates two different images on the retinas of both eyes). In the following I will discuss these four non-pictorial depth cues:

Motion Parallax: Motion parallax (or also referred to as motion perspective[19]) refers to the fact that if the observer is moving, the projections of stationary objects on our retinas move as well. Importantly, the motion of these projections is strongly dependent on the distance of the stationary object, which makes motion parallax an important depth cue. Consider the example of a train ride. When looking out of the window, nearby objects "fly by" in a blur while distant objects closer to the horizon seem not to move at all. While motion parallax is considered to be one of the most important depth cues for animals [70], Cutting & Vishton state that for humans the effective range of motion parallax for perceiving depth diminishes rather quickly with increasing distance [38].

Convergence and Accommodation: Convergence describes the angle between the two optical axes of the eyes, which changes with the distance to the focused object. For an object very close, e.g. in front of our nose, the convergence angle is very large as the eyes have to rotate inwards to foveate on the object. When the object moves farther away, the convergence angle decreases until it reaches 0 degrees, and the two eyes are aligned parallel, e.g. when focusing towards the horizon. Accommodation refers to the reflexive bending of the eye's lens, which aids in focusing the light reflected from an object onto the back of the retina. The amount that the lens must bend to focus an object's retinal image differs depending on the distance of the object. Light reflected from objects that are closer require more focusing and hence a fatter lens; light reflected from objects that are farther require less focusing and hence a thinner lens. Thus, the perceptual system can use information about bending of the lens to infer depth. Both the convergence angle between the eyes and the accommodation of the lenses are controlled by eye muscles, and the amount of contraction in the muscles can be used as a depth cue, with higher contraction signaling a closer object. Both cues are naturally linked[20], however, their usefulness decreases quickly as the eyes become effectively parallel for fixation distances larger than six meters and the variation in the convergence angle is rather limited for fixation distances larger than 0.5

---

[19]Both terms refer to the same concept or same cue, however, motion parallax is often used to describe the relative movement of the projections of several stationary objects depending on a moving observer, while motion perspective describes the motion of a whole field of such objects, c.f. [65, 38].

[20]While in natural environments both, convergence and accommodation are tightly coupled, this is not the case for many virtual reality setups providing a stereo image. In fact this can pose a problem, as one has to focus on the screen distance (e.g. in HMDs or large immersive screens) and converge to a virtual object which is located in front or behind the screen. Thus, both sources of information are conflicting, usually resulting in misperceived depth. This will be discussed in detail in section section 2.2.2.

meters [154]. Similarly, accommodation alone seems not to be very useful for perceiving absolute depth but can be used for perceiving relative depth (see for example [134] for a study investigating the usefulness of these extraretinal cues in isolation). According to Cutting & Vishton, the effectiveness of these depth cues declines very quickly for distances beyond two to three meters [38].

Binocular Disparity and Stereopsis: Binocular disparity is a term that describes the difference in the position of an retinal image between the left and right eye due to the horizontal separation of the eyes. Based on the difference in the retinal images, it is possible to perceive depth (i.e. stereopsis). The difference in the position of the retinal projections between the two eyes diminishes with object distance. Closer objects have larger differences in the positions of the retinal projection between the two eyes; farther objects have smaller differences between the right and left retinal projections. Binocular disparity is considered to be one of the strongest depth cues (see for example [13], demonstrating that disparity matching alone is sufficient for guiding a reach) and provides a compelling impression of depth and a reliable source of relative depth (but not necessarily absolute depth, see [154] for discussion). For absolute depth perception, it would be necessary to assume that the distance between the eyes (IPD - inter-pupillary distance) and more importantly, the convergence angle is known, see [38], or the information of disparity needs to be scaled otherwise, see [154]. Because of the decreasing disparity between the two retinal images, binocular disparity is most effective in the "near-field" and the effectiveness diminishes linearly with increasing distance [38].

For an overview, all discussed depth cues including their effective ranges are summarized in **Figure 2-1** (schema adapted from [160], content based on [38]). Considering both discussed groups of depth cues, it is clear why one could say that there is actually a wealth of information available to perceive depth in our surrounding environment, or more specific: to reconstruct depth from a two-dimensional image on the back of our retina. Thus, given a visually rich environment, humans have multiple sources of information to perceive depth (i.e. distance), and most importantly, all of these cues can also be presented in virtual environments to provide observers with information about distance. In fact, different findings suggest that distance perception becomes more accurate as more depth cues become available [100, 154]. Nevertheless, how all these cues are effectively combined to perceive distance in a visually rich environment is still an open question. Although several models have been proposed (e.g. Clarke & Yuille distinguish between 'strong' and 'weak' fusion [of cues] models [29], see [21] for an example for strong fusion and [102] for an example for weak fusion), Proffitt & Caudek argue that none of the models can account for all the empirical results that have been observed and that the question how cues are effectively integrated is a "tough problem" [152].

Furthermore, distance perception seems not to be only a question of how the different cues are integrated. Research during the last decade indicates that not only the availability and reliability of depth cues influence the perception of distance. Other sensory information and the environmental context may also play a role in perceiving distance. For instance, multiple

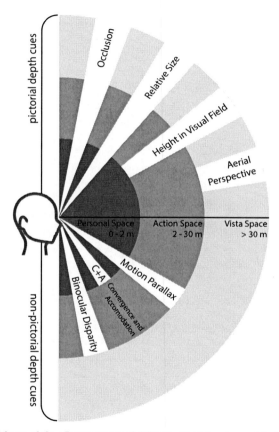

Figure 2-1: Schema of the effective ranges of different pictorial and non-pictorial depth cues in personal, action and vista space. The depth cues are selected from [38], the layout of the schema is adapted from [160].

studies have demonstrated that specific environmental contexts can influence perceived distance even when in a full-cue environment [182, 103, 220]. In the work of Witt and colleagues, they demonstrate that despite the presence of different depth cues, perceived distance was influenced by the size of the environment where the experiments were conducted (e.g. a hallway with a boundary — a door — and one end with no nearby boundary, see [220]). Similarly, Lappin and colleagues have shown that distance judgments differed whether the experiment was conducted in a lobby, a hallway or an open lawn, even though all depth cues were available [103]. Thus, these studies provide some evidence that even in a full-cue environment, the environmental context, although not providing specific depth cues to the indicated distance, can have an additional effect on perceived distances.

Another line of research argues that bioenergetic costs and even intention can influence the perception of distances. For example wearing a heavy backpack makes hills look steeper and increases the perceived distance [156]. This effect was replicated by Witt and colleagues [219], and the researchers also argue that this effect is action-specific and dependent on the intent of the observer. Thus, Proffitt concludes that perception is "is influenced by three factors: the visually specified environment, the body, and the purpose", see [152]. There is much more research supporting such a view on perception (see [155] for a detailed overview of the conducted research). However, such an influence of personal variables like the body and action-specificity is also questioned by other researchers, see for example [80, 115, 46] and this debate is still ongoing, yet beyond the scope of this dissertation[21]. Nevertheless, the described research and corresponding debate illustrates nicely, that even today the process by which humans perceive distance, is not well understood. Thus, while the basics of human distance perception are relatively well understood there remain many open questions.

2.1.3 Measurement Methods and Performance

The previously discussed wealth of depth cues and other information (i.e. personal variables, environmental context etc.), which contribute to perceived distance, and the adherent complexity of how this information might be integrated and combined to a coherent percept of distance pose a challenge for measuring perceived distance. Because of this complexity and also the cognitive nature of human perception, it is impossible to *directly* measure (visual) distance perception as we simply do not have access to other's subjective experiences. Although distance perception involves some covariants, which can be measured directly (e.g. the convergence angle between the eyes) the integration of all other information contributing to perceived distance is a process in the brain which cannot be directly observed or measured. However, it is possible to *indirectly* measure distance perception by using measures involving cognitive and motor responses to given controlled stimuli. Thus, it can be inferred what the observer's specific perception of the environment might be. During the last decades of research many different measures to as-

---

[21]Specifically the body-centered theory of perception which was recently presented by Proffitt & Linkenauger [155] triggered a heated debate about how our perception (and distance perception) works. To cover this debate is beyond the scope of this dissertation, however for the interested reader I recommend the criticism from Firestone [54] and the corresponding answer from Proffitt [153], to gain some insight of the debate how perception works and why this is not an easy question to answer.

sess perceived distance have been developed, which can roughly be divided in three groups (see [115] and [160] for recent overviews): verbal estimates, perceptual matching tasks, and visually directed actions (commonly called action-based measures).

The first group of verbal estimates and magnitude estimation represents very common and traditional measures. Also such verbal estimates are usually very fast and easy to use as the observer is asked to verbally report the egocentric distance to a specific target in a specific unit (e.g. meters or feet) or in the context of a given magnitude [114]. The advantages of this type of measure are obvious, as it is straight forward and easy to understand. However, some researchers argue that verbal estimates may be influenced by cognition. That means that a verbal response might not only be driven by what the observer actually perceived, but could also be influenced by prior knowledge of the observer, deductive reasoning and working memory capacity, which could distort the measure [114]. While verbal estimates are usually quite accurate for distances in the near field (intercept of 0), they are usually underestimated for larger distances (with a mean slope of 0.8, see Loomis & Philbeck for a comprehensive overview of studies [115]).

The second group are perceptual matching tasks, where the observer is for example asked to match a given extent to another seen extent (this can be for example matching the egocentric distance to an exocentric interval, see [117, 116], or matching an exocentric distance interval to a seen egocentric distance [110]). While this method is thought to be less influenced by cognitive effects, there might be other undesired side effects, depending on how the matching task is designed. Research provides some evidence that there might be a perceptual distortion, resulting in exocentric distances being perceived differently from egocentric distances (usually larger), and this distortion may also be present in matching tasks, thus introducing a bias in this measure (e.g. [116, 117], see [64] for special effects in IVEs). Another variant of such a perceptual matching task is the bisection task, where the observer has to indicate the midpoint of an egocentric distance interval. If the object size is known, the bisection task can yield accurate results [165]. In general, the advantage of perceptual matching tasks is that they are usable in scenarios where it may be not feasible to use action-based measures (e.g. in a CAVE or LSIDs) and in comparison to verbal reports they are not so easily influenced by cognitive effects.

Finally, the third type of measures consists of action-based measures for perceived distance. This group is also commonly referred to as visually directed actions [119, 115]. In general, the method can be described as follows: The observer sees a target at a distance, is then blindfolded and performs an action towards the target. The most common action-based measure for measuring egocentric distance perception is direct blind-walking, where the observer sees the target, is blindfolded and then attempts to walk to the previously seen target. Using this measure, it has been shown that humans are able to estimate distances up to 25 meters accurately without systematic errors [119, 71, 166], given that other factors like walking speed [165], strategy and other cognitive factors (e.g. counting steps) can be controlled. To circumvent those issues, triangulated walking has been developed, where the observer instead of walking blindfolded towards the target directions turns a specific angle and walks in this new direction. After a short time (usually based on a signal) the observer stops, turns back in the direction where he believes the target to be. From the new turning angle the observer either walks towards the target, or based on this angle the perceived target location can be calculated. Estimates obtained using this measure are considerably accurate up to a distance of 20 meters, although, according to Loomis & Philbeck, the variability compared to direct blind-walking increases [115]. Another measure closely related to direct blind-walking is timed imagined walking, which in principle follows the same method than direct blind-walking. However, instead of actually walking blindfolded towards the previously seen target, the observer closes his eyes and imagines walking to the target. With a stopwatch, the observers can estimate how long it would take to walk to the target. Using the natural walking speed of the observer as a baseline, the distance estimate can be calculated. The advantage of this measure is the minimized space requirements, however, this measure may also include some additional variability as the imagination task is not equally easy for every observer. Nevertheless, timed imagined walking has been shown to be similar in accuracy to direct blind-walking [71, 148]. Further action-based measures include throwing to the previously seen target which yields similar estimates as direct blind-walking (e.g. [175]), or using affordance measures where the action is not executed (the action component is thought to be task relevant) but used to estimate for example the distance between two poles (e.g. can you walk through these two poles without turning your shoulders?) [63].

The following table summarizes the different discussed measures and lists representative work using these measures to assess perceived distances in the real world and in virtual environments[22]. In general, all measures used in the real world to assess distance perception have been adapted for the use in virtual worlds, however, not all measures are usable for all VR setups (see [160] for a detailed overview):

---

[22]While covering the most important measures in the context of distance perception, this list of examples is not exhaustive. There are many other measures and variations thereof, for example also indirect measures, which use the relationship between perceived size and perceived distance [69] to assess distance perception, however this is beyond the scope of this dissertation. For the research presented in this dissertation, a representative measure from the group of the action-based and verbal measures were chosen.

Measure	Example	References
Verbal reports	"Look at the target and report in meters/feet how large the distance is."	[130, 143, 128, 10, 165, 109]
Direct blind-walking	"Look at the target, then close your eyes and walk to the remembered target location."	[34, 71, 92, 215, 119, 114, 101, 98, 230, 165, 113, 143]
Triangulated blind-walking	"Look at the target, then close your eyes, turn and walk. When told, turn towards the remembered target location."	[61, 113, 143, 202]
Pointing	"Look at the target, then close your eyes, turn and walk. When told, turn and point to the remembered target location."	[55, 56, 57]
Blind-throwing	"Look at the target, then close your eyes and throw the bean bag to the remembered target location."	[175, 187]
Perceptual matching	"Match the distance indicated between the two reference objects to be equal to the distance between you and the target."	[116, 117]

Considering Variability

The previous section demonstrates that there is a large variety of different methods to measure perceived distance. Furthermore, distance estimates often vary depending on the measure used, for example verbal estimates are usually underestimated in comparison to a blind-walking measure, at least with increasing distance to the target [115]. However, variability is not only dependent on the chosen measure. Even for direct blind-walking, one of the most common measures, which is considered to yield accurate real world estimates out to a distance of approximately 25 meters [115], this is only true when considering group averages. Distance perception is highly variable between individuals, thus, when someone refers to accurate estimates, one usually refers to the average of the tested sample. This means that when blind-walking, some observers walk too short and others "over-walk" the indicated distance [116], which leads to an accurate average of the tested sample. This applies for distance perception in the real world and also in different virtual worlds. Thus, it is usually necessary to test a large enough representative population of observers to decrease the inherent variability in distance measures. Furthermore, it has also been suggested that even the instructions of how to perform the task can have an influence on the estimated distance (e.g. [222, 203]) or that the measurement protocol can have an influence on the estimated distances [71]. Therefore, it is necessary to have a clear experimental protocol and to strictly follow it across all participants in an experiment. In summary, distance estimates can vary due to various factors (e.g. the used measure, protocol, available cues etc.). If all factors are carefully considered, appropriate measuring methods will yield representative results, which are usually accurate in the real world (e.g. for direct blind-walking, see [119]). Nevertheless, egocentric distances are perceived accurately in the real world with sufficient cues, but are usually underestimated in virtual worlds. What contributes to this underestimation if all of the mentioned factors influencing distance estimates are considered?

2.2   Distance Perception in Virtual Environments

The question how humans perceive distances has not only received a lot of attention in the real world, but has also triggered a lot of research efforts to understand how humans perceive distances in virtual worlds[23]. Many applications using IVEs heavily rely on a veridical perception of the depicted virtual space (see section 1.1.2), thus, it is not surprising that one of the first studies investigating distance perception in virtual worlds was motivated from an applied architectural background for simulating different spaces. In one of the first studies on distance perception in IVEs (1993), Henry & Furness asked twenty-four architects to tour through "either a real museum gallery or a real-time computer generated model of the same gallery under one of three increasingly inclusive viewing conditions i.e. looking at a monitor, viewing through stereoscopic head-mounted displays without and with head-position tracking" [76]. They found that in all simulated (VR) conditions the dimensions of the gallery were underestimated compared to the real world condition, and interestingly the condition using the head-tracked stereoscopic head-mounted display (one could assume that this condition was technically the closest to the real world condition) was most underestimated. Since then, this underestimation of distance in virtual worlds has been observed in numerous studies investigating different factors, which are likely candidates to contribute to this underestimation of distance (e.g. [202, 34, 175, 101, 114, 4, 82, 109, 133], see [160] for an extensive overview). The following sections highlight related research attempting to find the cause for the commonly observed underestimation of distance in IVEs. Moreover, related research trying to counter this underestimation will be discussed.

---

[23]In principle all discussed pictorial cues, which are used to perceive depth in the real world can also be simulated in virtual environments. For the non-pictorial cues there are some limitations, especially for accommodation and convergence depending on the used VR system, which will be described in detail in section 2.2.2.

2.2.1 The Underestimation of Distance

There is converging evidence, that distances are generally underestimated in IVEs, and this observation is not limited to specific hardware setups such as head-mounted displays. However, the amount of underestimation can vary by quite large amounts, depending on the measure and VR hardware used [160]. For example, a direct blind-walking measure of perceived distance, which yields veridical results in a real world setting (e.g. see [119]), is underestimated by as much as 50% of the distance intended from the programmer in IVEs (tested distances were 2, 6 and 19 meters, see [91]). Another study from Durgin and colleagues observed that participants walked only 65% of the intended distance of 2 - 8 meters in IVEs [45], and again another study which tested distances from 2 - 5 meters found 81% [212]. Most notably, the same measure was used in two studies for comparison reasons and the reported means suggest veridical performance in the real world (i.e. close to 100%, see [212, 91]). Similarly, a study from Thompson and colleagues used triangulated walking as measure and found it to yield accurate results in the real world (i.e. 95%), however they found drastic underestimation in the IVE (only 44% of the intended distance ranging from 5 - 15 meters, see [202]). Moreover, verbal estimates also yield different underestimations in IVEs. While verbal estimates in the real world are usually linearly compressed with increasing distance (i.e. the slope is 0.8 with an intercept of 0, see [115]), they can also be drastically underestimated in virtual environments (i.e. 62.32% of the intended distance in a low quality graphics room, 77.91% in a high quality room, see [101]). However, other results show that verbal estimates in a high quality IVE are close to veridical (e.g. 92%, see [109]), indicating a large variation, depending on the used hardware, software and measurement protocol. In addition, how exactly the measurement task was performed (see [160] for an overview of different measures and differences in instructions) may play an important role as well as the specific underestimation of an observer[24].

Nevertheless, a recent review considering distance estimation studies in VR from 1993 to August 2012 (78 articles in total, 30 articles which were considered for calculating the mean) found that on average egocentric distances are underestimated by about 26% with respect to the intended (modeled) distance [160]. However, even today the reason for this underestimation is not clear; although, many factors which could contribute to this underestimation have been investigated. The reason for the observed underestimation is still unknown, and researchers have speculated that underestimation of distances in virtual environments may be due to a variety of factors including hardware errors, software errors and errors of human perception or a combination thereof [87]. The factors investigated include technical issues or hardware specific issues, missing or conflicting depth cues, the quality of graphics, distortions and calibration issues.

---

[24]In fact, there is a large variability between individuals concerning underestimation of distances in virtual worlds. While some observers walk only 30% of the intended distance, others walk close to veridical, even in an IVE.

2.2.2 Technical Factors

The key difference between the real and virtual worlds is that the observer perceives the virtual world always mediated through some display technology (e.g. HMDs, large screen displays, CAVEs, powerwalls etc.). Thus, specific technology might have certain influences on the virtual world, which in turn could contribute to the underestimation in IVEs (see also [160] for an overview). In this section I will discuss related research trying to investigate factors, which are often specific to the used VR hardware and are thought to influence distance perception in IVEs.

The Influence of Hardware

Different technical factors or certain limitations of the used VR technology were expected to be a reason for the underestimation of distances in IVEs, and most of the research on these technical aspects were focused on HMDs, as it was (and still is) widely used in distance perception studies. Thus, likely candidates contributing to the observed underestimation in IVEs concern factors specific to HMDs, like the usually restricted field-of-view (FOV), the inertia (weight) on the head or the fact that the users need to wear something on their heads. Research investigating the influence of the FOV found that this has no impact on the perceived distance, at least if the observer was allowed to move/rotate the head for scanning the floor where the target was placed and the surrounding environment (see for example [34, 92]). However, when using a mock HMD in a real world setting, which resembled the same FOV and weight as the actual HMD (a nVisor SX60 from NVIS in this case), distance was significantly underestimated using direct blind-walking as a measure, although by a lesser amount compared to the usual underestimation in IVEs [213]. Interestingly, when using a headband, which replicated the inertia and weight of an HMD without restricting the FOV, Willemsen and colleagues found no reliable underestimation in the real world [215].

Another research group conducted similar experiments and confirmed the findings from Willemsen and colleagues, by showing that direct blind-walking estimates were significantly underestimated in the real world when wearing a "see-through" HMD (see [71]). Nevertheless, similar to Willemsen et al., their observed effect does not fully account for the whole underestimation, as shown by a direct comparison of using the HMD in the real world compared to a condition of using this HMD in the virtual world. In addition, they also tested an augmented reality condition where targets were virtually placed on the real floor and distances were compressed by a similar amount compared to the HMD condition [71]. In summary these studies suggest that FOV restrictions alone are not responsible for distance underestimation, but can in combination with the inertia and weight of an HMD contribute to the underestimation of distance in HMD-based virtual environments. Further research needs to be conducted to fully understand the contribution of each of these factors to the distance underestimation in HMD-based VR, especially given that recent research suggests that the field of view can influence perceived distance alone by a certain amount (see Jones et al. [84], where they compared 150° FOV with a simulated 60° FOV and found a significant improvement in the distance judgments, albeit still underestimated by a large amount).

Although HMD-based IVEs are most often used in distance perception studies (see [160] for a comprehensive comparison), the underestimation of distance has also been investigated across other VR devices, like large screen displays (LSIDs) or CAVEs (e.g. [33, 86, 87, 121, 148]). Several studies report also an underestimation of distance (e.g. [146, 148, 90]), only one study reported comparable results to performance in the real world [163]. The fact that a similar underestimation of distance is also often found across different LSIDs and not only in HMD-based IVEs, provides evidence that the underestimation of distance is not limited to specific hardware like HMDs and is a more general phenomenon for VR.

Missing or Conflicting Depth Cues

While usually all previously described pictorial depth cues (see Section 2.1.2) can be simulated in virtual worlds, non-pictorial depth cues, i.e. motion parallax, accommodation and convergence, and binocular disparity can be conflicting or even be missing in virtual worlds, depending on the VR system. For example, motion parallax can be missing if the head of the user is not tracked. Although motion parallax is quite effective for perceiving relative depth in the real world (at least for distances in action space, see [38]), the effectiveness of this non-pictorial depth cue in IVEs is not fully understood and different studies provide inconclusive results. For example Creem-Regehr and colleagues have shown [34], that head movements are important for accurately perceiving distance in the real world when using a mock HMD with a restricted FOV, which indicates that motion parallax is necessary for veridical distance perception. However, this finding may not necessarily be due to added motion parallax; it could be a result of using information gained from near-to-far scanning of the ground plane to inform distance perception (see e.g. [227]). Furthermore, other research has suggested that motion parallax is a rather weak cue for determining distance in IVEs. For example Beall and colleagues tested the influence of motion parallax in a VR display by altering the gain of the head movements, and they found no influence on perceived distance, which indicates that there is a "relatively weak effect of absolute motion parallax (and of optical flow in general) in determining visual scale" [10]. Similar conclusions were also drawn by Luo and colleagues, who tested the effect of motion parallax on size constancy in a CAVE and found that "motion parallax, either produced by the virtual environment or by the observer, might not be a significant factor in determining [...] performance" [121] (similar results were also found by Piryankova in a LSID, see [146]). Thus, due to the lack of empirical evidence it is likely that the lack of motion parallax is not the cause for distance underestimation in IVEs. Nevertheless, this does not mean that head tracking is unnecessary in IVEs, as it has been shown that it is very important for immersion and the feeling of presence in the virtual world (i.e. the *sense of being in* the VE, see for example [16, 135] for further information).

While the availability of motion parallax usually depends on the VR system (i.e. head tracking vs. no head tracking), all common stereoscopic VR systems have the same problem concerning accommodation and convergence. Using such VR systems, the virtual image of the computer generated environment is always mediated through some display technology. This can pose a problem for the observer, who is looking at an image but seeing a virtual object, as the image where the virtual world is displayed and the virtual object are usually not in the same place. The observer accommodates to the display, which is usually at a fixed distance, so it is focused while the eyes converge to the distance of the virtual object (see [77] or [13] for a detailed explanation). While the accommodation distance is dependent on the VR system, convergence changes either if the observer moves or if the virtual object moves. Some researchers argued that this mismatch can heavily disturb perception and as such can have negative effects on the perception of virtual worlds in general [13], because in the real world accommodation and convergence are tightly coupled and coincident. In fact, Bingham and colleagues have shown that in a reaching task the participants overestimated the reaching distance by approximately 15% compared to a real world task [13]. They argued that convergence is usually "pulled" towards accommodation, thus in their case they observed relative overestimation, as the virtual image was displayed at a focus distance of one meter and the targets were placed at a distance of 70% of the maximum reach of a participant. Another study by Hoffmann and colleagues also investigated the effect of such a mismatch by using a volumetric display [77]. They also found an effect of an accommodation-convergence mismatch on perceived near-space distances, however this effect was relatively small. They also found that this mismatch can cause visual fatigue and suggest that this effect can be reduced by increasing the distance to the display. In fact, they state that "focus cues have less and less influence as the distance to the display increases; there should be little influence beyond 1 m" [77]. In HMDs, this is usually realized by using collimated optics, which can simulate a focus distance to the virtual screen at infinity, thus the visual fatigue is reduced. According to Bingham and colleagues [13], convergence should be pulled towards accommodation, thus when using collimated optics with a focal point at infinity, perceived distances should be pulled towards infinity and consequently be overestimated. In summary, the mismatch between accommodation and convergence can have a negative impact on visual performance and cause visual fatigue, however, empirical evidence is limited to reaching space research, and overestimation was observed, not underestimation [13]. Hence, this mismatch can have an undesired impact on perceived distances, but it depends on where the observer has to focus and more research is needed to fully understand the consequences of such a mismatch.

The third non-pictorial depth cue, binocular disparity, is known to be a strong depth cue in the real world [38], however, its influence on perceived distance when using stereoscopic displays is less clear. Multiple studies have compared monoscopic viewing conditions with stereoscopic viewing conditions (in the real world and VR) and have found no reliable difference between the distance estimates [34, 214, 146]. However, other studies have found influences of stereopsis on a size adjustment task in a CAVE [121, 122], where size estimates were better (and less error prone) when the scene was seen in stereo. Another study investigating performance in reaching space found similar influences, where a perceptual matching task in reaching space was better when it could be performed with binocular compared to monocular vision (see [13]). However, it is important to consider the different tested ranges throughout the discussed studies. While all studies investigating action space (i.e. the space out to around 30 meters) found no reliable difference, the studies investigating personal space (i.e. the space within approximately

2 meters around the observer)[25] found an influence. As binocular disparity is most effective in near space [38], these conflicting results could be due to the different ranges tested throughout the experiments. In fact, the only distance where Piryankova and colleagues found an influence of monoscopic vs stereoscopic viewing conditions when using a LSID, was the nearest distance of 2 meters and the difference was not significant for the next tested distance of 2.50 meters [146]. Overall, missing binocular disparity cues (i.e. no stereo image) can influence distance perception, but mainly near space distances. Furthermore, this does not explain why distances are underestimated when stereoscopic viewing conditions for example in HMDs or stereoscopic LSIDs are provided.

The Quality of Computer Graphics

The first VEs to study perception in virtual worlds were rather limited in their graphical quality and were often consisting of rudimentary content like a ground plane and very simple objects, without realistic texturing. Thus, Loomis & Knapp [114] suggested that the observed underestimation in IVEs may originate from the low quality rendering of the VE, more specifically because "the rendering of the scenes used [in our experiments] is lacking subtle but important visual cues (e.g., natural texture, and highlights)", see [114]. Informally, they also observed a difference when a real world image of the real environment was projected into the HMD (via mounted cameras), which appeared "much more realistic in terms of distance and scale than [our] computer-synthesized virtual environments" [114].

Because of this hypothesis, some researchers attempted to investigate whether the quality of graphics may play a role in the observed underestimation of distance in IVEs. Specifically, Willemsen & Gooch [212] compared high-quality stereo panoramic photographs of a hallway with a virtual model of the same hallway. While distance judgments were slightly better in the photograph condition, this difference was not reliable (i.e. non-significant) [212]. Willemsen & Gooch stated that they "believe that the quality of graphics does not matter as much as previously thought" [212]. Similarly, Thompson and colleagues investigated the quality of graphics by providing their participants with either stereoscopic panoramic images, a low quality virtual model or a simple wire-frame version of this model [202]. When tested with triangulated blind-walking using a HMD they also found no difference between those conditions, which were all similarly and significantly underestimated compared to the real world condition. Thus, the quality of the rendering of the virtual environment may not be the cause for the observed underestimation in IVEs. However, this hypothesis was revisited by Kunz and colleagues [101], using different measures (i.e. verbal estimated and direct blind-walking). They found that while direct blind-walking was not different in a high-quality virtual room compared to a low-quality virtual room, verbal estimates were significantly different (62.32% of the intended distance in the low-quality room and 77.91% in the high quality room). Furthermore, research by Leyrer and colleagues reported similar results for a high-quality IVE [109]. Using a high-quality replica of a real office including light-maps in their experiment, they found verbal estimates to be 92% of

---

[25]Bingham and colleagues investigated only reaching distances out to 70% of the maximum reach of a participant, see [13], and Luo and colleagues used a virtual bottle for the size judgments, which was placed at a maximum distance of 9.5 feet, i.e. approximately 2.90 meters, see [121].

the intended distance. Similarly, Phillips and colleagues [144] found also a significant improvement in the distance judgments using direct blind-walking by using a photorealistic rendering of a real room compared to a low-quality wire-frame like model of the same room. However, in this case, the added information by using high quality textures (i.e. texture gradient etc., see section 2.1.2) could be the reason. In addition, the experiment was conducted in the same room the IVE depicted, which could have side-effects on perceived distance[26].

In summary, there is no concluding evidence whether the quality of graphics has an influence on perceived distances in IVEs. Furthermore, Renner and colleagues point out that some of the methodologies used might be confounded [160]. For example comparing stereo panoramic images with a 3-dimensional VE can also provide different cues to the observer (e.g. motion parallax in the case of the IVE compared to the images), even when the eye height of the observer and his inter-pupillary eye distance (IPD) were taken into account. Conversely, the influence of impoverished IVEs (like wire-frame models, e.g. [144]) does not rule out the possibility that sophisticated high resolution graphics including shading, lighting and natural texturing etc. would have an impact on the perceived distance in IVEs. Further studies using high-end graphics available in computer games would be necessary to further investigate the influence of the quality of graphics on perceived distances in IVEs.

Geometric Distortions and Calibration Issues

In general, VR technology often tries to display to the observer a view of the scene which resembles very closely how the scene would look in a natural environment. However, depending on the technology used, different distortions can occur in this process. In the literature usually the following distortions are mentioned: *FOV distortions, radial distortions, pitch distortions,* and *distortions of the stereo base* (IPD). While many of these distortions can be corrected for (e.g. radial distortion, see [98, 96]) others can be avoided with a careful calibration of the equipment (e.g. a distorted pitch angle [98, 96]). Nevertheless, researchers have investigated how these distortions may impact the perception of distances in IVEs.

One of the more recently investigated distortions is the FOV distortion. The result of such a distortion is either minification or magnification, which can occur, when the FOV of the virtual cameras in the VE (also called *geometrical FOV* or *GFOV*) does not exactly match the FOV of the display (*display FOV* or *DFOV*) where the image of the virtual cameras is rendered. Minification occurs if the GFOV of the virtual cameras is larger than the DFOV and magnification if the opposite is true (GFOV < DFOV). While measuring the correct DFOV of a large planar projection screen is trivial, this can pose a problem for curved screens or in HMDs. For example, especially for HMDs, the provided information of the manufacturer for the DFOV can be erroneous (see e.g. [98, 193]), and if one trusts these values, minification or magnification is the result. Regarding distance perception, it has been shown multiple times that this distortion has an effect on perceived distances (e.g. [97, 98, 230, 18, 85]) using direct blind-walking. However, not all measures seem to be affected the same way. For example, Zhang

---

[26]This is actually in line with the idea of a so-called *transitional environment*, a technique trying to counter the observed underestimation in IVEs, which will be discussed in the next sections.

and colleagues [230] reported that a direct blind-walking measure was affected by minification, however verbal estimates were not. Similarly, Walker and colleagues did not find any difference due to minification in an affordance judgment [204]. Interestingly, Steinicke and colleagues [193] investigated whether users are sensitive to these GFOV to DFOV mismatches and found that in both experiments, the participants set the GFOV closely to the DFOV indicating that this is the most natural representation for an observer (at least for near space interactions). Furthermore, Kellner and colleagues tried to carefully calibrate the GFOV separately for each user, nevertheless they still found significant underestimation in a distance judgment task using blind-walking [85].

Other research has investigated whether a pitched environment has an impact on perceived distances in IVEs. Specifically, for tracked HMDs (or tracking glasses for stereoscopic displays), it is not always guaranteed that the orientation of the HMD is aligned with the optical axis of the display or that tracked glasses are calibrated correctly, which may result in a pitched up or down environment with respect to gravity, see [98]. Using an HMD, Kuhl and colleagues investigated whether pitching the whole world up or down by 5.7° by manipulating the virtual cameras has a negative impact on perceived distances. However, they did not find any difference in the distance estimates due to the pitched environment[98][27].

Another distortion, which is specifically present in HMDs is radial distortion (also called pincushion distortion) due to the optics used in an HMD to enable a reasonable FOV and to allow the user to focus on a distance, which is not directly in front of the eyes. However, other devices, which use sophisticated optical systems (e.g. photo cameras) always have a certain degree of distortions. Most noticeable in HMDs is the radial distortion, also often referred to as pincushion distortion (see for example [98, 96, 211, 221]). The effect of such a radial distortion is that "points near the edges of the image are magnified more than those near the center" [98]. Thus, every line in the image, which is not crossing through the center of the lens will appear slightly curved, and the more the line is away from the center of the optics, the more curvature it will have. However, if the degree of radial distortion is known, a correction can be implemented to correct for this distortion[28]. Nevertheless, Kuhl and colleagues investigated whether such a distortion due to the optics of an HMD has an impact on perceived distances in IVEs. They found no difference in the distance estimates, whether radial distortion was corrected or not.

Finally, distortions may be introduced by using a fixed distance between the two virtual cameras (left eye and right eye) instead of adjusting this distance to the IPD of the corresponding user. However, research results are inconclusive whether this introduces distortions, which can affect the perception within IVEs. In reality, it is usual to use a common distance between the virtual cameras for all users, mainly for reasons of simplicity, although for example Drasic &

---

[27]Important to note here is the fact that in their work Kuhl and colleagues pitched the whole environment. That means all the relative angles in the environment stay the same, but are altered with respect to gravity. However, real world research suggests that visual information is dominant for determining the eye level, see for example [124, 228]. Thus, while it is well known that the angle of declination below the horizon (i.e. the angle between the target and the eye level) is important for perceiving distances (see also [137] and section 2.3.2), it is not surprising that a pitch with respect to gravity does not yield differences in the distance estimates.

[28]Today, such an altering of the image geometry or *warping* can also be achieved directly through the driver of the graphics card, which is then calculated directly on the GPU. This is an easier and computationally more efficient correction, than correcting this distortion using software in the rendering pipeline.

Milgram stated that even small deviations in the distance of the virtual cameras from the IPD of the user can result in large distortions [43]. Yet, other researchers argued that a false setting (compared to the IPD of the user) can even be necessary to address stereo fusion problems or to create more depth for flat scenes [210], or proposed dynamic disparity adjustments to generate compelling virtual stereo scenes (e.g. [207]). However, empirical evidence on how such a mismatch between the distance of the virtual cameras and the IPD of the user is sparse. Using a binocular depth matching task, Rosenberg [174] has found that the performance was drastically improved when the distance was changing from 0 to 2 cm. However, there was no significant improvement beyond a 2 cm distance between the virtual cameras [174]. Similarly, Kellner found no effect on distance estimates whether the virtual scene was rendered with a camera distance of 6.5 cm[29] or an adjusted distance based on the measured IPDs of their participants [85]. Similarly, Willemsen and colleagues used the same method and did not find any differences except for their largest tested distance (i.e. 15 m), where the measured IPD was set as the distance between the virtual cameras and the participants walked further compared to the standard distance of 6.5 cm [214]. Furthermore, Bruder and colleagues found that changes in the distance between the cameras had only a small effect on distance judgments "when set in direct relation to the tested range of GFOV gains" [18].

In summary, all discussed distortions do not explain the magnitude of distance underestimation in IVEs. Specifically, radial distortion due to the optics in an HMD and a pitch distortion (pitching of the whole environment) due to a bad calibration do not influence perceived distances in IVEs. In contrast, minification and magnification do have effects on perceived distance, thus, careful calibration of properties like the GFOV is necessary, to ensure that there are no negative side effects on perceived space in virtual worlds. Furthermore, the stereo base can have an influence on perceived distance, however only under certain circumstances. In general, because of these distortions, a careful calibration of the VR technology is necessary, but even in carefully calibrated systems underestimation of distance is present (e.g. [98]).

2.2.3   The Availability of Depth Cues

The discussed investigated factors potentially contributing to the observed underestimation of distance in IVEs included the main factors investigated in the literature (see for example [160] for a comprehensive overview). However, there are still other factors like the availability of different pictorial depth cues, which are also important. As stated before, in principle all pictorial depth cues can be provided within a VE, and a lack thereof can also have comparable effects to the real world. In fact, many virtual worlds are cue reduced to provide controlled stimuli to the observers, e.g. just presenting a single object on a ground plane. This paucity of pictorial depth cues may have an impact on perceived space in virtual worlds. For example, it is well know that if the availability of pictorial depth cues in the real world is reduced, the accuracy of distance perception is also reduced (e.g. [143, 142, 100]). Similarly, in a simple VE, generated by using a stereoscope on a monitor and systematically varying the available depth cues,

---

[29]The IPD of humans usually varies between 5 to 7 cm, and a distance of 6.5 cm is a common distance between the virtual cameras used throughout many VR studies.

Surdick and colleagues have shown that different cues have different impacts on the distances matching estimates [198], with perspective cues (linear perspective, texture gradient) being the most important depth cues. Furthermore, other research has investigated full-cue vs. sparse-cue environments, and found that the performance in a perceptual matching task was better (see [86, 122]) in the environment providing more pictorial depth cues. These findings in combination with the wealth of research indicating the importance of specific pictorial depth cues and environmental context in perceiving distance (e.g. [182, 74, 65, 38, 227, 220, 103]), it is obvious that virtual worlds need to provide certain features to enable the observer to adequately perceive distance. Nevertheless, even in complex, full-cue environments, underestimation of distance can still be observed, thus underestimation of distance in IVEs can likely not be fully attributed to missing pictorial depth cues.

2.2.4 Attempts to Counter Underestimation of Distance in IVEs

The main research focus concerning distance perception in IVEs during the last decade(s) was on understanding the perceptual process underlying space perception, which also includes finding the reason for the underestimation of distance. However, as discussed before, many of the likely candidates to cause this underestimation have been shown to not fully account for the observed amount of underestimation. Thus, other researchers have attempted to compensate for the distance underestimation with different approaches, to enable the observers a perception of the IVE, which is close to what was intended by the content designer. In the following sections, I will discuss some of the underlying ideas of these approaches, as they vary strongly in how they suggest that distance perception in IVEs can be altered. For example, one idea is to *alter or warp the present depth cues* in the virtual image (e.g. by minification, see [97, 98, 230]) to improve the perception of distance, while others tried to employ a *feedback paradigm* [162, 205, 130]. This essentially means, that the observer in a VE receives feedback about his actions from executing them in the IVE or gets feedback about his performance, thus improvement over time is observed. A similar idea is to provide a VE, which is the same as a real environment with which individuals have prior experience, because that knowledge might transfer into the IVE [82, 144]. Finally, another line of research argues that the observed underestimation of distance might be caused by the fact that the user is often not represented appropriately in the virtual world, thus researchers have suggested that the present misperception in IVEs can be alleviated if observers have a virtual self representing them in the IVE. In summary, all of these ideas and the corresponding approaches aim to provide the observer with an experience that is close to what is intended by the designer, and in the following sections I will highlight some examples of these approaches and will also discuss their advantages and disadvantages.

Altering Depth Cues

As discussed in one of the previous sections, different geometric distortions, specifically the GFOV, i.e. the field of view of the virtual cameras capturing the VE, can have a large impact on perceived distance, if they are not calibrated well (e.g. [97, 98, 230, 18, 85]). However, for example work from Kuhl and colleagues suggest that exactly this fact can be exploited to counter the commonly observed distance estimation in IVEs. More specifically, their work has shown that minifying the virtual environment by altering the GFOV, which effectively scaled the imagery by a factor of 0.7 relative to the baseline condition (i.e. rendering the graphics with the specified GFOV according to the used HMD), can reduce or even eliminate distance underestimation [97, 98]. While this research was only using direct blind walking as response measure, recent results suggest that minification influences verbal reports and direct blind walking differently [230], as verbal responses were not affected by the manipulated GFOV.

Zhang and colleagues argue that this difference is desirable as verbal reports are usually also underestimated in the real world [230], thus their finding with blind-walking, yielding a close to veridical performance and underestimated verbal responses, may closely resemble performance in the real world. Nevertheless, it is not clear yet, why those measures are affected differently by a minification, as this technique usually alters many important cues to distance, namely binocular disparity, optic flow, the visual angles of every given object, linear perspective, familiar size and the angle of declination below the horizon, which should all have a similar influence on verbal estimates and blind-walking measures. Moreover, due to the change of the visual angles, size perception should also be affected by providing a minified image to the observer. Further research is necessary to investigate what happens to perceived space in general and not only distance using this approach and why different measures yield different results following drastic changes to the available visual depth cues. From an applied perspective it might also be interesting to have an approach where measures are affected in a similar way, because of the many diverse applied scenarios where IVEs are assessed often very differently (e.g. verbally, interactive, action-based etc.). Important to note is also, that the aforementioned work from Kuhl and colleagues tested only one specific manipulation for all participants (i.e. a minification based on altering the GFOV to scale the environment by a factor of 0.7, see [230, 98]). Thus, considering the previously discussed variability, this means that individuals may be differently affected by such a manipulation to the GFOV, because the manipulation is not based on the individual underestimation but the group as a whole. Thus, a further interesting study to investigate the effectiveness of this approach would be to provide every single participant with a specific GFOV instead of a fixed chosen value, which is tailored to the individually experienced underestimation. If their findings hold true when testing individuals, this would be a promising approach, however further research is necessary to fully investigate the possible side effects due to altered cues on different measures and the perceived scale of the environment.

Providing Feedback/Adaptation

Borrowing the definition from Mohler [129], *feedback* can be described as "sensory information that stimulates one or more of the five senses (vision, audition, touch, smell, taste) or proprioceptive and vestibular information that indicates the extent to which the individual's desired effect was accomplished" (see also[177]). Furthermore, this feedback can be either intrinsic or extrinsic, where intrinsic refers to the observer directly sensing from actions in the environment (e.g., vestibular information, visual information) or extrinsic, which refers to feedback received from an external source to corresponding actions of the observer (e.g. verbal corrections - assume for example a trainer coaching a player, see also [129] for more information). Based on this variety of feedback, which humans experience all the time in their daily life, humans can easily adapt their performance and perception to varying stimuli, as long the possibility to experience interaction within an environment is given (see e.g. [75]). An example indicating the adaptability of the human visuo-motor system from over a century ago is the experiment from Stratton, where he used prism glasses to turn his visual image of the world upside down [197]. After a while he calibrated to this image, so that the world did not seem to be reversed. Thus, the idea to use this ability of the human visuo-motor system to adapt to the environment to counter distance underestimation in IVEs with appropriate feedback or the possibility for adaptation is obvious. Therefore, some researchers investigated whether different forms of feedback can help to counter the observed underestimation in IVEs.

The study from Witmer & Sadowski is one of the first studies providing feedback within an IVE to improve distance perception [218]. To provide feedback, they asked their participants to open their eyes after walking blindfolded towards a target. Thus, they could see where in relation to the target location they stopped, which would allow them to adapt their walking in the next trial. However, they did not find a reliable improvement following this feedback, and a reason for this could be that they only used 15 trials throughout their experiment, which may not be enough as adaptation effects likely increase with the number of actions performed during the adaptation phase and not with the length of the adaptation phase (see for example [53]). In a whole series of studies Richardson & Waller instigated the influence of feedback on perceived distances more thoroughly [162, 161, 205]. When the participants of one experiment received explicit feedback about the modeled distance in a training session between the experimental trials, the participants' performance using a blind-walking task was veridical in the post-test compared to underestimated in the pre-test. Furthermore, also implicit feedback changed the perceived distance: when the participants were given the possibility to interact with the environment (i.e. walking with vision to the target or until a stop signal is given) the blind-walking measure afterwards yielded nearly veridical performance [162]. In addition, walking to the target without vision and only providing an auditory signal when the target is reached, significantly improved the distance estimates in a follow-up study [205]. Yet, providing simulated optic flow, which would occur when walking to the target, did not improve the distance estimates. Similar to the research of Richardson & Waller, research from Mohler and colleagues also demonstrated that walking to the targets with continuous vision, terminal visual feedback or walking without vision with an auditory stop signal improved the distance estimates [130].

However, recent research suggests that also for a feedback paradigm there might be differences depending on the measure used. For example a recent study from Altenhoff and colleagues investigating performance in reaching space when providing visual and haptic feedback (i.e. pretest, feedback session, posttest), suggests that while the action-based measure (here a reach) was affected by the feedback, verbal estimates were not, although they were obtained along with the performed reach [6]. The authors argued that the feedback might have been specific for the action (or more specifically the perception for action), while perception for cognition may require a different feedback paradigm, to allow the observers to adapt to the new distances. In summary,

47

providing feedback seems to be an effective tool to counter distance underestimation, however, it has also some drawbacks. First of all, providing feedback requires time and actions performed within the VE, which is often not feasible in different scenarios. Second, many applications in VR (for example training applications) require that the results are transferable to the real world, which might be a problem using a feedback approach to correct distance estimates. For example Waller & Richardson have shown, that feedback within the VE improves distance perception, but can have adverse effects on judgments in the real world (i.e. misperceived distances in the real world after veridical performance in the virtual world, see Exp 1 in [205]). Such aftereffects of adaptation due to feedback are also well known in the real world. For example after adapting over time to throw accurately to a target in the real world while wearing prism goggles, the same target will be missed after taking off the prism goggles [53]. Such aftereffects [53], also called carry-over effects [6] or transfer effects [218] may limit the usefulness of feedback and adaptation to counter distance underestimation in VEs.

Replicas & Transitional Environments

Another technique to reduce the underestimation of distance in IVEs is the use of replicas [82, 83, 144] and/or transitional environments (e.g. [192]). In their studies, Interrante and colleagues discovered that the distance underestimation in IVEs is drastically reduced, if that VE is a high-fidelity replica of the actual real environment where the observer is located during the experiment [83, 82]. Another study further investigating this phenomenon found that this effect can only be observed when the replica features photorealistic texturing; in a wire-frame model no improvement of the distance estimates was found. This led the authors to speculate that the quality of graphics may have an impact on perceived distance in certain circumstances [144]. Thus, replicas may be used to improve distance perception estimates, but only if it features high-fidelity graphics.

Based on these findings, Steinicke tested the concept of a transitional environment [192]. They used two different virtual environments in their study, a high-fidelity replica of their laboratory and a virtual city, which could be entered through a portal in the virtual replica of their laboratory. They found that distance estimates in the virtual replica of the room where the participants were doing the experiment, were much improved compared to the typical underestimation of distance in IVEs, replicating the work from Interrante and colleagues (i.e. [82, 83]). Furthermore, when the replica, or in this case transitional environment, was shown before the participants entered the virtual city, the distance estimates were better compared to experiencing the virtual city first and then the virtual replica of the lab [192]. However, while replicas alone seem to improve distance estimates in IVEs, their usability in applied scenarios is quite limited, because for many applications using VR technology the goal is to simulate a space, which is not easily available or expensive; this is why VR is used in the first place (i.e. for flight simulators etc.). While, the idea of transitional environments seems promising, further research is necessary to quantify the improvement, and whether the improvement is dependent on certain conditions.

Adding a Virtual Avatar or Self

Some researchers also suggested that the underestimation of distances in IVEs originates from the fact that the body of the user is usually not represented within virtual environments. This mainly applies to HMD-based IVEs, which immerse the user into the virtual world and block out the real environment including the user's own body. One real world experiment conducted by Creem-Regehr and colleagues tested whether it is important in the real world to see one's own body, specifically the own feet. They hypothesized that this missing information could lead to errors in distance judgments [34]. However, when they occluded the participants' vision to their feet and their lower body by having them wear a collar-like apparatus, they did not find any reliable difference in the distance estimates.

However, the importance of adding a virtual self to the IVE has been pointed out already for other reasons. For example Slater & Usoh argue that a virtual self-representation can help to improve the feeling of presence (i.e. *being there*), which in turn might alter how we perceive virtual worlds [183, 14]. Furthermore, other researchers proposed that the body might be central for the act of perceiving [9, 217, 150][30], which would argue for the importance of a virtual self-representation in a virtual environment. Thus, Mohler and colleagues suggested that providing the user with a view of one's own body might be helpful for either providing grounding in the virtual world by providing a scale, with which one could measure the environment or by providing a visual-motor coupling between the visual self and the performed actions [132, 133]. In fact, experiments from Mohler and colleagues have shown, that if the user is provided with a self-animated virtual self, distance estimates improved compared to a condition where no virtual self-representation was available [132]. Supporting these findings, Phillips and colleagues have shown that a self-animated avatar significantly improved the distance estimates in a non-photorealistic replica of a real room [145]. Similarly, Ries and colleagues have shown that a tracked avatar also improved distance perception, however, a static avatar did not. They argued that their results were due to an increased sense of presence in the IVE [164]. Nevertheless, they pointed out possible confounds in their methodology: participants walked through the tested hallway before they saw the VE, which could have an impact on the distance judgments, and their participants in the control condition did not wear the same motion capture equipment as did the participants in the self-animated avatar condition [164]. However, recent work from Mohler and colleagues suggests that as long the avatar is self-animated it does not matter whether the avatar is co-located or seen from a third-person perspective, in both cases the distance estimates were very close to veridical. In addition, even a static self had an impact on perceived distances, regardless of a first or third-person perspective [133].

Nevertheless, there are also results in the literature, where a self-animated avatar did not have an impact on perceived distance (see e.g. [127, 111, 109]). While McManus and colleagues point out multiple reasons why their self-animated avatar did not have an impact on the perceived distances, like the use of a mirror where participants immediately felt "this is not me" or the

---

[30]Such a body-based approach to perception is often referred to as *embodied perception* or the *functional approach to perception* (see [155] for a specific example of this theory). Because a sufficient discussion of these contemporary theories about visual perception is beyond the scope of this dissertation, I recommend the interested reader [155, 9, 217, 150] for further information about embodied perception theories.

short exposure time with the avatar [127], it is important to note that in the case of Lin and colleagues no underestimation of distance was found [111]. Consequently, it is clear why they found no difference between the various avatar conditions. Furthermore, in recent work from Leyrer and colleagues, the self-animated avatar only improved perceived distance when it was taken into account how much the participants felt that the virtual avatar was representing themselves in the virtual environment [109]. Thus, in summary, preliminary evidence indicates that avatars can improve perceived distance in virtual environments, although the requirements for this to happen are not fully understood. Further research is necessary to investigate how the user must be represented in the virtual world that this representation has the desired effect on perceived distances. Moreover, providing the user with a fully-animated self-representing avatar is currently not a trivial task. It requires expensive motion capture equipment, highly refined software, sophisticated 3-D models of the human body with a rigged skeleton, all of which require a great deal of money, time and specialized expertise. Nevertheless, providing self-animated avatars to counter the underestimation of distances in IVEs might be a promising venue for further research.

2.3 The Relation between Eye Height and Perceiving Space

In human perception, not only are the previously discussed visual depth cues important for visual perception, but additionally eye height and eye level (c.f. section 1.3) play an important role in allowing humans successful environmental interaction. Specifically, it is well known that eye height (also in combination with the eye level) is used to perceive heights of objects, affordances, and distances, all of which are required for interaction with a constantly changing environment. In the following sections, I will describe how eye height is important for determining these percepts, and specifically why eye height is important to perceive distances in real and also in virtual environments.

2.3.1 Object Height and Affordances

Eye height is important for visual perception, and this has been recognized for some time. For example, Alberti [3] experimented with the role of eye height and linear perspective in drawings already in 1436. Similarly, the architect Le Corbusier noted in 1955 that "the eyes are placed at a height above the ground variable according to the size of the person, this being the determining factor of perception" (see [106]). In fact, Warren & Whang point out "that architectural drawings are often drafted from a station point at the eye height of the client, so that the objects in the scene appear properly scaled", see [208]. This can be explained by the well known *eye height ratio* (also known as eye height scaling, see for example [155]), which describes that if an observer is standing on an approximately flat ground plane the eye level (in combination with the horizon) can be used to determine the heights of objects if they are standing on the ground plane. Thus, the height of objects is always specified as a ratio of the observer's own standing eye height, also often referred to as the *eye height unit* [208][31].

In his dissertation work, Sedgwick provided the first formalization for eye height scaling with respect to perceive object height [178]. In a flat, empty environment, the visible horizon is always on the same level as the observer's eye height, a concept that he termed the *horizon-ratio relation* [179]. Even when no explicit horizon is visible, i.e. in a room, the horizon is defined implicitly via several other sources, e.g. by the focus of expansion or bifurcation of optic flow. Objects in the visual field are of a height that is of some proportion of the visible horizon (defined by the eye height of the observer), and that proportion does not vary as a function of the object's distance from the observer. As a result, if one knows his eye height, s/he can determine the height of objects by determining the proportion of horizon that the object occludes. For example, if an object's height reaches halfway from the ground to the horizon, then the object is of a height that is half of the observer's eye height. Different experiments have shown, that this eye height scaling (or eye height ratio) is used to perceive the heights of objects in different real environments and also VEs. For example, Wraga has demonstrated the use of eye height scaling for object height across different postures using a false floor paradigm[32] [225]. Similarly, Dixon and colleagues have demonstrated that the same eye height scaling is used in immersive and non-immersive VEs [41].

Furthermore, it has also been shown that eye height or more specifically eye height scaling is used to scale affordances. According to Gibson [67], the perceived environment can be described in terms of affordances, which can be defined as possibilities for action on an object, given the structure of the environment in relation to the action capabilities of the observer. For example, a rigid surface at knee height affords sitting or stepping on; whereas, an object at shoulder height does not. Therefore, affordances are dependent on the action capabilities of the observer, which in turn are related to the relevant dimensions of the body. Thus, eye height should be important to scale affordances. Empirical evidence supports this notion. For example Mark demonstrated that eye height is used to determine whether one can sit on a given surface height or whether one can step on given stair heights [123]. Similarly, Warren & Whang have shown that eye height is used to determine whether the observer could pass through an aperture [208] and Stefanucci & Geuss have shown that eye height is used to scale whether an observer can pass under a horizontal barrier without ducking [189], providing further evidence for the importance of eye height for perceiving our environment.

---

[31]See Warren & Whang's work on eye height scaling [208] or Sedgwick's important work on the horizon [178] for the exact mathematical description how the eye height ratio can be used to determine the size of objects in principle independent of distance to the object.

[32]Wraga used a moveable false floor which could not be seen by the observers. If eye height scaling would be used for perceiving object height, the same object should be perceived as bigger when the false floor is raised. Exactly this was observed by Wraga [225], indicating that eye height scaling is used to determine the height of different objects in the environment.

2.3.2 Perceiving Distances using Eye Height

Eye height is not only important to perceive the height of objects or to scale affordances, but recent research suggests that eye height is fundamental to perceive distances in our surrounding environment. Sedgwick [178, 179] proposed that the angle of declination below the horizon (AoD) to a target on the ground in combination with the (known) eye height (EH) of the observer can be used to determine distances (d) following the equation $d = EH/tan(AoD)$ (see **Figure 2-2**).

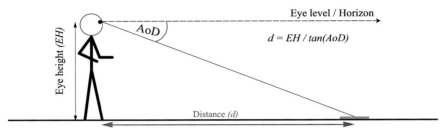

Figure 2-2: Egocentric distance perception using eye height and the angle of declination below the horizon to an object on the ground.

Ooi and colleagues have provided empirical evidence supporting this idea [137]. By using prism goggles to manipulate the angle of declination below the horizon, they demonstrated that the angle of declination in combination with eye height is likely used to determine distances. Furthermore, they showed that following adaptation the perceived eye level was altered, which in turn changed the angle of declination to the target and had an impact on the judged distances. Thus, by using one's eye height and the corresponding angle of declination, observers can determine egocentric distances using the illustrated relationship [137]. Other studies have also tested this hypothesis, and found similar results. For example Messing & Durgin conducted a study in VR, where they effectively altered the angle of declination below the horizon by manipulating (lowering) the virtual horizon by 1.5°, which reduces the angle of declination to a given target [128]. Following this manipulation, verbal and blind-walking estimates were overestimated compared to a baseline, supporting the angle of declination hypothesis [128]. Similarly, a real world study seeking to manipulate the visual horizon (under severely degraded vision) found a similar influence as would be predicted by the angle of declination hypothesis [159]. Rand and colleagues provided their participants with a raised horizon under severely degraded vision, and as would be predicted, found underestimation of distances compared to a baseline condition where the visual horizon was unaltered [159]. This compelling evidence about the importance of the angle of declination below the horizon in combination with eye height has even led researchers to the provocative hypothesis about "the role for angular declination in the perception of distance; namely, that angular declination is the only functional cue [to distance] extracted within the time frame of a typical eye fixation when to-be-localized targets are floor-level and outside of one's immediate space", see [62]. While their results did not support this very prediction, they show that the angle of declination provides "information about egocentric distance even on the very first glimpse", suggesting that it is a very powerful cue [62].

Surprisingly, while many researchers have provided compelling evidence that the relationship between eye height and the angle of declination is used for perceiving distances in different environments (real and virtual), they only focused on one aspect of this relationship — the angle of declination. Nevertheless, without eye height in the equation, this relationship does not work. Interestingly, in the literature investigating the angle of declination hypothesis, many researchers only refer to eye height as "assuming that the observer's eye height is known" (see for example [137]). However, how eye height is "known" or more specifically determined is still an open question. Warren & Whang suggest that it is informed by intrinsic information[33] because extrinsic alternatives (i.e. accommodation and convergence, binocular disparity and motion parallax) "are problematic" [208]. Similarly, Mark describes eye height as "intrinsic information" [123]. Thus, how eye height is determined remains unknown and will be investigated in this dissertation to understand the perceptual consequences this might have on distance perception in virtual environments and whether eye height is a factor, which can be used to counter distance underestimation in IVEs. While the information to specify eye height in the real world is usually coincident (the potential sources of information are tightly coupled in the real world) this is not true for different VR setups. Depending on how eye height is calibrated or even manipulated, different sources of information (e.g. what is visually seen in the virtual world) could indicate a different eye height from that of the physical eye height of the observer, which might have, according to the angle of declination hypothesis, different consequences on perceived distances.

---

[33]Warren & Whang used the term intrinsic information when they hypothesized what information is used to scale affordances. However, they never specified what this intrinsic information actually is they refer to, except that they use the term to also describe the eye height ratio.

Chapter 3

Investigating how Eye Height is Informed and Corresponding Hypotheses

3.1 Motivation

The question how eye height is informed has been around since almost 30 years, when Warren & Whang speculated about the different alternative sources of information, which could be used to inform eye height [208]. However, during the last decades, no empirical research has tried to find the answer to this question[34]. In contrast, different researchers provided compelling evidence that the angle of declination is a very powerful cue for perceiving distances in real and virtual environments [137, 128, 159, 62]. However, the angle of declination can be used to determine absolute distance only in combination with (a *known*) eye height. Thus, how eye height is informed is not only interesting from the view of perceptual psychology, but especially from an engineering view regarding VR. While in the real world all sources potentially specifying eye height are usually tightly coupled, this is not true for different virtual worlds. The virtual eye height is easily manipulated, and can also be a potential source for errors (e.g. no head tracking and a fixed virtual eye height, or insufficient calibration), depending on what information is used to determine eye height. In this chapter I will describe the motivation for the presented research in this dissertation from both views, the theoretical motivation and the engineering motivation. They are tightly coupled, as for applied purposes the perceptual theory must be understood to investigate the potential effects of eye height on perceived space in IVEs and IVEs make it easier to study perception.

The work presented in this dissertation is relevant for those who seek to improve the usefulness of IVEs and to understand how certain perceptual aspects like eye height influence how

---

[34]Here it is important to consider the definition of eye height used throughout this dissertation, namely the distance from the eye with respect to the ground surface (or eyes to the feet). Recent research investigating the *"eye height"* above a support surface (i.e. the distance from a table to the eyes) suggests that this specific *"eye height"* is determined by using stereo cues, see [139, 31]. Nevertheless, the eye height unit of the seated observer in front of the support surface (i.e. the eye height to the ground) can still be informed by different information, and it is not clear what this information is.

IVEs are perceived. Furthermore, this work is also relevant for psychologists interested in human perception, specifically in distance perception. In the following sections I will describe the perceptual and applied motivation along with the corresponding research questions and hypotheses this dissertation aims to investigate.

3.1.1 Perceptual Theory

Human eye height is fundamental to perceive many important aspects of our surrounding environment (see section 2.3), yet how humans inform their eye height is still an open question. During the last decades, different researchers have speculated about this information without any empirical investigation as of yet. Warren & Whang speculated that *intrinsic* (what I consider to be body-based information) information is used to inform eye height or in their case the eye height ratio which is used to scale affordances [208]. In contrast, Sinai and colleagues conducted experiments, where they asked their participants to stand on an elevated ground surface of two meters height and judge their eye height to the lower ground surface and estimate distances to targets also placed on this lower ground surface. Eye height was drastically overestimated in this case and distances were also overestimated in their experimental setup. Thus, they concluded, that "it is likely that the adult observer's eye height [...], being a constant most of the time, leads the visual system to internalize it as implicit knowledge (a yardstick)" [182] (see **Figure 3-1** for an illustration of their setup).

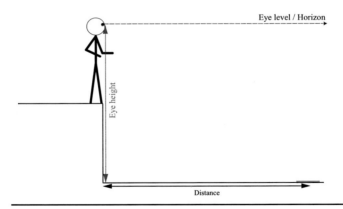

Figure 3-1: The setup used from Sinai and colleagues. The indicated eye height to the lower ground plane was drastically overestimated as well as the distances. Figure adapted from [182].

A third option is the use of visual information to determine eye height throughout changing environmental contexts, as has for example been shown for the perceived eye level [124, 195, 196, 228]. However, it is important to note the distinction between eye height (i.e. the perpendicular distance from the eyes to the ground) and the concept of eye level, which could be considered mutable and more akin to line of sight, or as Wraga put it, as "the projection of the observer's line of sight into the environment" [225]. Eye level is important for perceiving the relationship between one's eye height and sizes and distances (i.e. horizon ratio, see for example [178, 179, 137]); whereas, eye height defines the size of the scale (also called eye height unit).

One notion in the field of visual perception is that visual information dominates over information from the other senses [158], and different studies have provided support for this notion (see for example [149, 73, 170, 171]). Thus, the assumption that also eye height might be informed by vision seems reasonable, especially given the fact that eye level seems to be primarily determined by visual information. While the eye level can be judged quite accurately in the dark by using body-based cues (e.g. the orientation of the head with respect to gravity), when no visual information is available [124, 195, 137], research for example from Wu and colleagues indicates that the eye level can be altered when the observer is provided with different optic flow fields. They argue that "when a discrepancy [between body-based and visual information] occurs, the internal setting is adjusted towards that defined by the environmental visual cues" [228] (see also [137, 32, 124] for similar results indicating a dominance of visual information over the information provided from other senses to determine the eye level). Thus, eye height could also be determined by visual information similar to the eye level. However, if this is the case, why did Sinai observe drastic overestimation in the obtained eye height judgments and distance judgments, which would suggest that eye height was not informed appropriately by vision with respect to the ground surface where the targets were shown? Of course, if vision is used for informing eye height, stereo cues likely play an important role in this process and given the setup of Sinai (see **Figure 3-1**) with an elevated surface of two meters height, the standing eye height of the observer with respect to the lower ground surface is likely not within the effective range of stereo cues. An alternative explanation would be the use of body-based cues to inform eye height. In the illustrated case, body-based cues might not be able to inform eye height with respect to the lower ground surface, which would for example be the case if you step for example on blocks which are resting on a ground surface (c.f. [123]).

Thus, different sources of information could be responsible for informing eye height. Investigating which source of information is actually used to inform eye height may help to better understand the perceptual process underlying distance perception. Evidence for using either visual information or body-based information to determine eye height would provide new insights into how the brain combines and uses information for a task which is fundamental for our survival. However, it would be surprising if it is not visual information, which is used to inform eye height, because one of the dominant theories regarding visual perception suggests that visual information is dominant over information from other modalities (e.g. [158, 149]). However, other findings challenge this view. For example others have argued that the body of the observer itself is central for perceiving our environment, and not the visual information present in the environment alone [155]. Therefore, if eye height would be informed by body-based cues, these findings contribute to the field of visual perception by providing further evidence that we perceive our environment not only by using primarily the visual modality.

3.1.2 Applied Problem Solving

Virtual reality technology can be considered a multi-purpose tool for diverse applications in various domains, e.g. training, prototyping, design, entertainment and research investigating human perception. However, for many of these applications it is necessary that the designed and computer-generated VEs are perceived as a replica of the real world. Many research studies have shown that this is not the case. As highlighted in the introduction, specifically egocentric distances are underestimated compared to real world estimates regardless of whether the virtual environment is displayed in a HMD or on a LSID. While the main reason for this observed distance underestimation is still unknown, virtual eye height might play a role in this commonly observed underestimation if not correctly calibrated (or manipulated) or might even be used to reduce distance underestimation depending on which sensory information is used to determine eye height.

Specifically, while in the real world usually all sources of information specifying eye height are naturally coincident, this is not necessarily true for IVEs for example presented via HMDs. Eye height can be visually different from the body posture of the observer, e.g. when the observer is physically sitting but seeing the IVE from a virtual standing eye height. Depending on how eye height is informed across various contexts, this mismatch has different perceptual consequences. I consider mainly two potential sources of information to determine eye height in this dissertation, namely visual and body-based information and both of these could also contribute to an internalized knowledge of eye height. The former is composed of optical information and the latter is composed of proprioceptive and vestibular information. Considering the angle of declination hypothesis for perceiving distances and for example the assumption that eye height is either informed by visual information or by body-based information, distance is likely perceived differently depending on the source of information used to determine eye height.

Suppose that observers assess their eye height by relying solely on visual information. If this were true, then observers should determine their eye height depending on the visual information specifying depth to the ground surface and this should vary depending on their posture or manipulations to the visual information. In other words, any discrepancy between body-based and visual cues in the specification of eye height should result in the ratio between eye height and the tangent of the angle of declination remaining invariant. In such a case, perceived distance would be constant even when visually-specified eye height and the corresponding angle of declination change (see **Figure 3-2**). Thus, differences between the physical and virtual eye height of the user should not have any consequences.

Alternatively, if eye height is determined via body-based cues, and there is a discrepancy between visually-specified and body-based eye height, the related visual angle from the different visually-specified eye height should be applied to the body-based eye height. Consequently, the angle of declination to the target changes with an increase in visually-specified eye height. In combination with an unchanged body-based eye height an increase in visually-specified eye height should result in decreases in perceived distance, whereas decreases in visually-specified eye height should result in increases in perceived distance (see **Figure 3-3**). Therefore, any discrepancy between the physical and virtual eye height of the observer might result in misperceptions of distances in IVEs, which in turn might also open up possibilities for manipulations to the virtual eye height to alter distance perception in IVEs (e.g. to reduce or even counter distance underestimation).

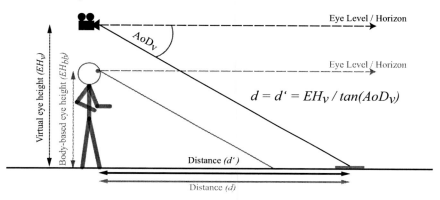

Figure 3-2: If eye height is informed by vision (EH_v) and continuously informed by visual information across various environmental contexts, the ratio between eye height and tangent of the angle of declination (AoD_v) and therefore the distance remains the same. **Note:** The camera symbol represents the manipulated visually-specified eye height in the VE.

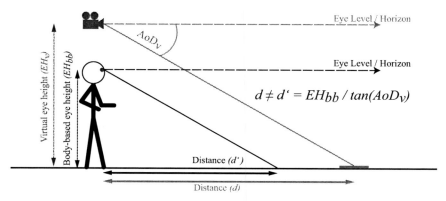

Figure 3-3: Prediction based on the use of a combination of the visually-specified angle of declination (AoD_v) and the body-based EH (EH_{bb}) of the observer regardless of the potentially displayed environment. In the case illustrated, underestimation of the distance is predicted, whereas for a lowered virtual EH overestimation of the distance is predicted. **Note:** The camera symbol represents the manipulated virtual EH.

Thus, how the observer determines his eye height, may either have no applied consequences, or far reaching consequences for perceiving distances in IVEs. Assuming that eye height is informed by body-based cues, the described underlying perceptual knowledge about the angle of declination hypothesis could be used to determine what impact for example a fixed eye height in a specific VR setup has on perceived distances. However, more importantly, if eye height is informed by body-based cues, eye height manipulations might be an easy and effective solution to reduce or even counter distance underestimation to enable users to perceive the IVE like intended by the content designer, without many of the drawbacks from the presented approaches in Chapter 2.

3.2 Research Questions and Corresponding Hypotheses

In the context of the presented theoretical and applied motivation multiple research questions arise. In the following, I summarize the research questions this dissertation aims to investigate and the corresponding hypotheses for the various conducted experiments, which are presented in Chapters 4 and 5. Some of these experiments attempt to answer multiple of the following questions or multiple experiments were conducted to find an answer to a single research question.

3.2.1 What Sensory Information is used to determine Eye Height?

Hypothesis 1: Eye height is informed by body-based cues. The first main research question in this dissertation aims to investigate what sensory information is used to determine eye height in a typical VR scenario. Despite the fact that many researchers have speculated about this information, to my best knowledge no empirical evidence for or against specific sources of information, which are potentially used to inform eye height to a ground surface, has been presented. However, this question is not only important to better understand the process of distance perception but can have far reaching implications for distance perception in IVEs as described in the section before. Despite the reasonable assumption that all sources of information could be used to determine eye height, I hypothesize that eye height is informed by body-based cues. As already pointed out by Warren & Whang almost 30 years ago [208], the alternatives (i.e. internalized knowledge or using visual information) are rather unlikely. From my perspective, the alternatives are unlikely for multiple reasons: Internalized eye height is unlikely, because our eye height can change very frequently given different environmental contexts. Of course the relationship between different eye heights and relevant actions is learned over time, so experience may play a role in specific circumstances. Nevertheless in many situations, humans need to be able to very quickly inform different eye heights to ensure our survival. Also the other alternative is rather unlikely: Visual information can specify eye height through different optical variables, nevertheless, the main visual depth cues which would be available to determine eye height, all yield poor absolute distance information, despite the popular notion that visual information is usually dominant. Thus, the body-based senses seem to be a likely and reliable candidate for informing eye height for perceiving distances in real and virtual environments.

3.2.2 Is Eye Height for Perceiving Distances informed by changes in Posture?

Hypothesis 2: When changing the posture, eye height is informed accordingly to ensure an unchanging visual environment. Regardless of what information is used to inform eye height in different environmental contexts, it needs to be flexible. We change our posture multiple times a day and yet, the perceived environment does not change. For example, when you sit on a chair and then stand up, the bookshelf across the room should still be perceived as having the same size and being at the same distance. Thus, eye height needs to be informed by changes in the posture (e.g. sitting vs. standing). Both main sources of information, namely visual and body-based would allow for such a necessary flexibility in determining eye height. By using different postures in different experiments, this dissertation aims to investigate whether IVEs are perceived differently using different postures or whether eye height is appropriately informed by changes in the body posture of the observer.

3.2.3 Is eye height in VR informed differently from eye height in the real world?

Hypothesis 3: The information used to determine eye height is similar in virtual and real environments. As described in Chapter 2 in this thesis, virtual worlds are often special in how they are perceived compared to the real world. Thus, one assumption might be that also eye height is informed differently within an IVE compared to the real world. One could for example argue, that the provided visual information in IVEs might not be reliable enough to determine eye height. Therefore, eye height could be informed differently across IVEs and the real world, according to the reliability of the present sensory information. This would also have practical implications: If a specific source of information to determine eye height would only be used in VEs, for example because the visual information is not reliable enough, it is possible that this reliability increases with improved VR technology. This in turn would limit the usability of the approach presented in this dissertation. However, I hypothesize that the source of information (likely body-based information) to determine eye height in IVEs is also used in the real world. Although no empirical evidence for this assumption is available, previous results from real world experiments could partially be explained if eye height is informed by body-based cues also in a real world context (e.g. [182, 123]).

3.2.4 Can Virtual Eye Height manipulations be used to Reduce or even Counter Distance Underestimation?

Hypothesis 4: Eye height manipulations are a valuable tool to reduce or even counter distance underestimation in IVEs. Based on the assumption that eye height is informed by body-based cues, the expectations are that perceived distances are overestimated when the visual eye height is lower than the actual eye height and underestimated when the eye height is raised. However, I also hypothesize that not only the direction is predictable but also the amount of under- or overestimation (i.e. predicting the actual perceived distances due to a manipulated visual eye height). Of course, human distance perception is variable, depending on the measure used and distance underestimation can also vary quite strongly between individuals. Nevertheless, when assuming that humans fully rely on their body-based cues to inform their eye height, I believe that the relationship between eye height and the angle of declination below the horizon to the target can be used to closely predict the changes in perceived distances due to a manipulation of the visual eye height in IVEs. Thus, if the individual amount of underestimation in a given IVE is known, it should be possible to manipulate the virtual eye height to reduce or even counter the observed individual underestimation in an IVE. Consequently, manipulations of the virtual eye height could be a promising solution to reduce or counter distance underestimation in IVEs on an individual basis, which is usable across many different applied scenarios.

Chapter 4

Sensory Information for determining Eye Height for Egocentric Distance Perception in Different Postures

4.1 Introduction

In this chapter, I present a series of studies designed to investigate what sensory information might be primarily used to determine eye height in the context of egocentric distance perception. However, investigating which sensory information is used to specify eye height is difficult as visual and body-based information specifying eye height is tightly coupled and both sources of information could be used to determine eye height. Specifically, it is not trivial in real world experiments to decouple the two sources of information in an ecologically valid way: This would require either 1) maintaining the same body-based cues while moving visual eye height above or below the physical eye height with respect to the ground surface where the distance estimates are performed, or 2) moving the body (and therefore the eyes), while preventing body-based cues to sense this change in eye height with respect to the ground surface where the distances estimates are performed (e.g. like in [182] where they used an elevated ground surface). Important in these examples, and for my definition of eye height, is to create situations, where visual and/or body-based eye height can be manipulated independently of each other with respect to the ground surface where distance estimates are performed.

However, in the context of near space and reaching paradigms, recent related research demonstrates that eye height (with a slightly different definition) can be easily manipulated using for example a table, and that recalibration to an altered table height is necessary for veridical reaching performance (see [31, 139]). Pan et al. [139] and Coats et al. [31] define eye height as "the distance of the eyes above the support surface (called eye height", which is in their case a table, while I refer to eye height as the distance from the eyes to the ground surface. While the mentioned work has elegantly shown that recalibration to such constantly changing eye heights above different support surfaces (e.g. table heights) is necessary, and that "this recalibration can be achieved using feedback information" [139], these studies do not decouple the two sources of information specifying eye height to the ground. A similar example in action space is the important work from Wraga demonstrating the use of eye height scaling in different postures for perceiving the size of objects by using a false floor paradigm (c.f. [225]). Important in this paradigm was not to decouple visual and body-based eye height, but rather to investigate whether observers calibrate the sizes of objects relative to the eye level, which varied according to changes in posture [225]. The manipulated floor could only be seen by the observers when they looked through the pin-hole to the objects, but not when looking directly down. Therefore, visual and body-based cues to eye height remained coupled. Thus, the eye height to the ground (defining the scale for judging object size) could have still been determined by visual or body-based information. Therefore, decoupling body-based and visual information potentially specifying eye height, according to my definition, is not a trivial task.

However, VR technology can provide a means for decoupling body-based and visual cues that specify eye height. Using this technology it is possible to decouple body-based and visual cues to investigate whether this dissociation influences perceived distances in VR. I used the angle of declination hypothesis [137, 178], which states that the eye height of the observer and the visual angle to the target (angle of declination below the horizon) is used to determine distances to objects, to make predictions about how each cue may influence perceived distance.

Reiterating the example from before, suppose that observers assess their eye height by relying solely on visual information. If this were true, then observers should determine their eye height depending on the visual information specifying depth to the ground surface and this should vary depending on e.g. their posture or manipulations to the visual information. In other words, any discrepancy between body-based and visual cues in the specification of eye height should result in the ratio between eye height and tangent of the angle of declination remaining invariant. In such a case, perceived distance would be constant, even when visually-specified eye height and the corresponding angle of declination change. Alternatively, if eye height is determined via body-based cues, and there is a discrepancy between visually-specified and body-based eye height, the related visual angle from the different visually-specified eye height should be applied to the body-based eye height. Consequently, the angle of declination to the target changes with an increase in visually-specified eye height. In combination with an unchanged body-based eye height an increase in visually-specified eye height should result in decreases in perceived distance, whereas decreases in visually-specified eye height should result in increases in perceived distance.

However, if eye height is determined by body-based cues, then such a system would need to be flexible enough to allow for a consistent perception of distance when the observer is standing, sitting or lying in a bed (c.f. [225]). Thus, the eye height used to determine distances should change according to changes in the body posture. To achieve a constant perception of the world the eye height unit could be internalized as a remembered eye height. Perceivers have experience with various postures and the perceptual system could learn the relationship between the different eye heights of such postures over time. Another way to assure perceptual constancy would be to determine eye height with respect to relative changes in the body posture in real-time and without the need for a stored representation of eye height based on prior experience.

4.2 Experiment 1: Manipulating Visual Eye Height in VR in a Standing Posture

In this first study, body-based and visually-specified eye height were decoupled using VR. Participants experienced a visually taller or shorter eye height while standing on a flat ground plane and estimated distances to targets, while they were not told that that the floor they saw in the VR scene was at the same height as the height of the physical floor they felt under their feet in the real world. Changes in visually-specified eye height should be coupled with the corresponding changes in the angle of declination. As a result, if perceived eye height is specified by visual information distance estimates should remain constant across different eye heights. However, if eye height is determined by body-based cues, then increases and decreases in visually-specified eye height should only influence the angle of declination with respect to determining distance, leading to compression of distances following an increase of visual eye height and expansion of distances following decreases in visual eye height compared to the baseline estimates.

4.2.1 Method

Ethics Statement

In this and all subsequent experiments presented in this dissertation, participants started by completing a written consent form. All experiments were performed in accordance with the 1964 Declaration of Helsinki and were approved by the ethical committee of the University of Tübingen. All participants were debriefed and informed of the purpose of the study at the end of the experiments.

Participants

Fifty-four paid (26 female) participants were recruited from the university community of Tübingen, Germany. All had normal or corrected to normal visual acuity and could fuse stereo displays. The age ranged from 18 to 64 years ($M = 29.13$).

Stimuli & Apparatus

The experiment was carried out in a fully-tracked free-walking space, 11.9 m × 11.7 m × 8 m high, with black walls and a black floor, see **Figure 4-1, A**. A virtual environment consisting of a flat ground plane without any familiar size cues was displayed through an Nvis nVisor SX60 head-mounted display (Nvis Inc., Reston, VA, USA) with a resolution of 1280 × 1024 pixels per eye (in stereo, see **Figure 4-1, B**). The head-mounted display (HMD) has a refresh rate of 60 Hz per eye and a contrast of 100:1. The field of view of the HMD is 60° diagonal, with a spatial resolution of approximately 2.2 arc-minutes per pixel. The HMD has collimated optics with a focal point at infinity, creating a virtual image, which appears to be at infinity rather than just a few centimeters from the face. This means that with the parallel display setup in the HMD, the eyes converge and accommodate towards a virtual plane at simulated infinity. According to Hoffmann and colleagues, this minimizes perceptual distortions due to an accommodation-convergence mismatch, because focus cues "have less and less influence as the distance to the display increases and there should be little influence beyond 1 m" (see [77]). The position and orientation of the HMD was tracked by a 16-camera Vicon MX13 (Vicon, Oxford, UK) tracking system. The environment included a visual horizon and a blue sky. To provide a correct visual horizon, a software correction was implemented to compensate for radial distortion due to the optics of the HMD (if uncorrected, the horizon would appear as a curve at the edges of the optics). The ground plane in the virtual environment was textured with a random stone pattern to eliminate familiar size cues while still providing linear perspective cues (through tiling) and texture gradient cues. The judged distances were indicated by an octagonal green disc with a radius of 21.5 cm and a height of 1.4 cm.

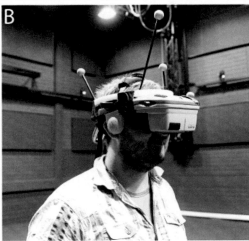

Figure 4-1: The technical setup: **A:** The fully-tracked free-walking space with a 16-camera Vicon MX13 optical tracking system. **B:** The HMD (NVisor SX60) used for the Experiments 1-4 in this chapter.

Experimental Design & Procedure

All participants received written and verbal instructions and were shown a meter stick with additional labels every 10 centimeters, until they indicated that they had a good representation of the length of the stick. The participants were randomly assigned to only one of three conditions (between-participants design), in which visually-specified eye height: (1) matched the body-based eye height *(0 cm)*, (2) was 50 cm lower than the body-based eye height *(–50 cm)*, or (3) was 50 cm higher than the body-based eye height *(+50 cm)*. The participants stood comfortably upright. They were not allowed to turn, bend, or lean forward or to the sides, nor were they allowed to deviate from their standing position (see **Figure 4-2**). In addition, in this and all subsequent experiments, the participants were not provided with (perceptual-motor) feedback from forward, backward or sideways locomotion to allow us to investigate, whether a change in visual or body-based cues specifying eye height influence distance estimates in isolation and without the opportunity to calibrate actions to the visual cues by providing feedback about the target distance (c.f. [162]).

Thus, the experiment started with a 5 minute training phase to familiarize the participants with the virtual environment and give them the possibility to explore the environment (station-ary — free head movements were allowed) and the manipulated eye height without any targets displayed. During this and the judgment phase all participants had the possibility to look down and were encouraged to do so. After the exploration phase, the target was displayed in the same environment at a certain distance, and the participants had as much time as they needed to judge the distance. When the participants indicated they were ready, the screen of the HMD was blanked; participants closed their eyes and turned their head 90° to the left and verbally reported the distance. Participants were instructed to report as accurately as they could in meters and centimeters. After reporting, the participants turned their head back, and following an indication of readiness from the participants, the next target was displayed. Participants completed 18 trials (4, 5 and 6 meters, each six times in a random blocked order).

4.2.2 Results & Discussion

I analyzed the verbal distance estimates using a repeated measures analysis of variance (ANOVA) with distance (4, 5, 6 m) and repetition (1–6) as within-subjects factors, eye height (–50, 0, or +50 cm) as a between-participants factor, and distance estimates as the dependent measure. As expected, distance was significant, with the estimates of distance increasing linearly from the 4 to 5 to 6 m distances, $F(2, 102) = 382.88, p < .001, \eta_p^2 = .88$. Overall distances were compressed, which is a well-documented phenomenon in VR using HMDs (c.f. Chapter 2 and see for example [114] for an overview).

The repeated measures ANOVA also revealed that the eye height manipulation had a significant effect on the estimated distances in the –50 cm ($M = 5.23, SE = 0.33$), 0 cm ($M = 4.04, SE = 0.18$), and +50 cm ($M = 3.17, SE = 0.17$) eye height conditions, $F(2, 51) = 18.85, p < .001, \eta_p^2 = .43$, suggesting that body-based eye height rather than visually-specified eye height is used to determine the egocentric distances if these sources of information are in conflict (see **Figure 4-3**). Post-hoc pairwise comparisons using Bonferroni

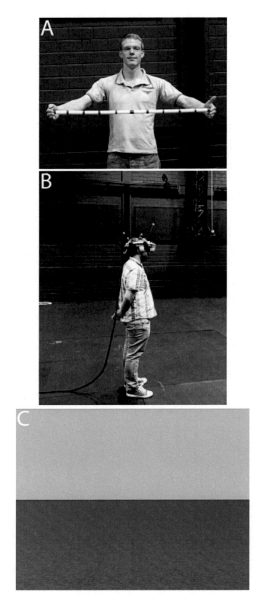

Figure 4-2: A: Experimenter showing the participant a meter stick with additional labels every 10 centimeters. **B:** Participant during the distance judgment task using the NVisor SX 60 HMD. **C:** The sparse-cue virtual environment used for Experiments 1-3.

correction confirmed significant differences between the –50 and 0 cm eye height conditions, $p = .003$, the 0 and +50 cm conditions, $p = .039$, and the –50 and +50 cm conditions, $p < .001$. In addition, there was an interaction between eye height condition and distance, $F(4, 204) = 10.84, p < .001, \eta_p^2 = .30$, with the differences between the eye height conditions increasing as a function of increase in distance, which is predicted by the body-based eye height hypothesis (or more specifically by the relationship between eye height and the angle of declination).

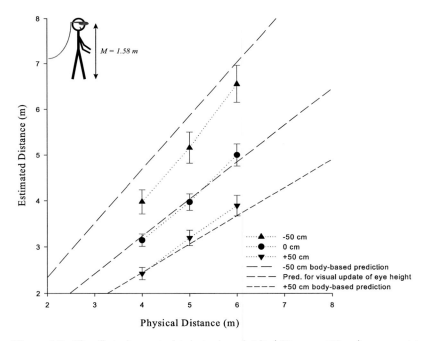

Figure 4-3: The effect of a manipulated visual eye height (–50 cm or +50 cm) on egocentric distances in a standing position in comparison to the respective baseline condition (0 cm). Error bars represent ±1 SE. The actual mean participant eye height in the experiment is depicted in the left upper corner. **Note:** (a) The predictions are shifted by the observed underestimation in the baseline condition to account for the usually observed distance underestimation in head mounted displays (in an ideal world, the 0 cm estimates would correspond to veridical performance). (b) If visually-specified eye height were used, there should be no differences and the prediction for visual eye height would apply for all conditions.

4.3 Experiment 2: Manipulating Visual Eye Height in VR in a Sitting Posture

The results of Experiment 1 suggest that body-based eye height is used to determine egocentric distances in a standing posture, if the information specifying eye height is in conflict. However, eye height needs to be flexible across various postures to achieve perceptual constancy [225]. I conducted another experiment using a standard sitting posture, which resulted in an approximately 50 cm shorter actual eye height compared to the standing eye height in Experiment 1. If body-based eye height is determined by body-based cues according to the posture, I would expect estimates in the 0 cm condition to be comparable to those in Experiment 1 (0 cm) and underestimation to occur in the raised (+50 cm) condition.

4.3.1 Method

Participants

Twenty-five paid (17 female) participants were recruited from the university community of Tübingen, Germany. All had normal or corrected to normal visual acuity and could fuse stereo images. Age ranged from 18 to 54 years ($M = 29.08$).

Stimuli & Apparatus

The same technical setup and virtual environment as in Experiment 1 were used. In this experiment, the participants sat on a standard chair with 44 cm sitting height (with a 44 cm long × 46 cm wide seat). The chair was positioned on the ground at the same location on the floor where the participants were standing in Experiment 1, see **Figure 4-4**.

Figure 4-4: Participant judging distances in the sparse-cue virtual environment in a sitting posture.

Experimental Design & Procedure

The procedure was the same as in Experiment 1, except that participants were seated. The participants were randomly assigned to only one of two conditions (between-participants design), either (1) a baseline condition where the visually-specified eye height matched the actual seated eye height *(0 cm)* or (2) a 50 cm raised *(+50 cm)* visually-specified eye height. I omitted the -50 cm condition for this experiment as the -50 condition situated individuals in a pilot study so close to the ground plane that, given a seated posture and a moving head (with varying eye height), eye height that was not always positive (as in above the floor). Participants were instructed to sit upright and not to bend at the waist or lean forward to obtain a better view of the target. The participants were allowed to rotate their heads freely. The participants did not receive any feedback about the accuracy of their estimates. Participants completed 18 trials (4, 5 and 6 meters, each six times in a random blocked order). The procedure for reporting the distances was the same as in Experiment 1.

4.3.2 Results & Discussion

Two participants were removed from the analysis, one for being more than 3 SD above the mean and another after her admission of being a specialist in this research area. Distance estimates were analyzed using a repeated measures ANOVA with distance (4, 5, 6 m) and repetition (1–6) as within-subjects factors, eye height (0 and +50 cm) as a between-participants factor, and distance estimates as the dependent variable. As expected, distance was significant, with distance estimates increasing linearly with increasing distance, $F(2, 42) = 371.68, p < .001, \eta_p^2 = .95$. There was a similar distance compression as in Experiment 1.

Supporting the hypothesis of using body-based cues to determine eye height, a repeated measures ANOVA confirmed that the distance estimates were significantly higher in the 0 cm eye height condition ($M = 3.69, SE = 0.13$) compared to the +50 cm condition ($M = 2.97, SE = 0.23$), $F(1, 21) = 7.67, p = .012, \eta_p^2 = .27$ (see **Figure 4-5**). In addition, there was an interaction between eye height condition and distance, $F(2, 42) = 3.34, p = .045, \eta_p^2 = .14$, with the differences between the eye height conditions increasing as a function of increase in distance, which is in line with the body-based eye height hypothesis. Furthermore, I also tested the converse prediction. If distance judgments would have been based on an internalized standing eye height, the +50 cm condition of Experiment 2 should yield similar estimates than those observed in the baseline condition (0 cm) of Experiment 1. However, an independent samples t-test confirmed, that they are reliably different, $t(27) = -3.61, p < 0.01$, supporting the idea that body-based eye height is determined by body-based cues according to the posture.

4.4 Experiment 3: Manipulating Visual Eye Height in VR in an Uncommon Prone Posture

The results of Experiments 1 and 2 suggest that visual information may not be dominant for determining eye height, if the sources of information are in conflict. However, these experiments do not fully resolve whether participants use an internalized eye height informed by experience of the posture or whether it is determined in real time according to body-based information. Standing and sitting are very common postures so experience in these postures could have informed eye height. To investigate whether experience is necessary to determine eye height, participants estimated distances in a less common posture: lying prone on a bed. If experience

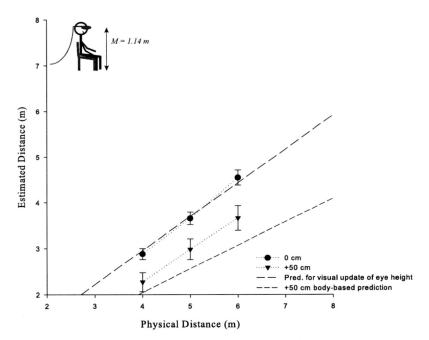

Figure 4-5: The effect of a manipulated visual eye height (+50 cm) on egocentric distances in a sitting posture in comparison to the respective baseline condition (0 cm). Error bars represent ±1 SE. The actual mean participant eye height in the experiment is depicted in the left upper corner. **Note:** (a) The predictions are shifted by the observed underestimation in the baseline condition to account for the usually observed distance underestimation in head mounted displays (in an ideal world, the 0 cm estimates to veridical performance). (b) If visually-specified eye height were used, there should be no differences and the prediction for visual eye height would apply for all conditions.

is important, I would expect participants to rely mostly on an internalized standing eye height. If eye height is determined by body-based information in real time, then the participants should use their body-based information from getting on the bed to specify their new eye height with respect to the ground surface.

4.4.1 Method

Participants

Forty-two paid (22 female) participants were recruited from the university community of Tübingen, Germany. All had normal or corrected to normal visual acuity and were screened for the ability to fuse stereo displays. The age ranged from 16 to 48 years ($M = 27.33$).

Stimuli & Apparatus

For Experiment 3, I used the same technical setup and virtual environment as in Experiment 1. Participants completed the distance judgments while lying prone on an adjustable hospital bed (model Evolution MA 2, Hill-Rom, Batesville, IN, USA), see **Figure 4-6**.

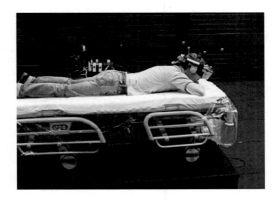

Figure 4-6: Participant judging distances in the sparse-cue virtual environment in a lying prone posture.

Experimental Design & Procedure

Participants started in a different room than the one in which the experiment was conducted. The participants received written and verbal instructions. To allow for lowering and raising the visually-specified eye height, while still being able to climb on the bed directly from the floor, it was adjusted to reflect the approximate seated eye height of the participant (adjusted by the experimenter before the participant entered the room). The experimenter showed the participants the meter stick, until they indicated that they had a good image of the stick in mind. The experimenter then guided the participants into the tracking space and instructed them to get on the bed and repositioned them to ensure that all participants had approximately the same lying position on the bed. After donning the HMD, the experiment began with the same exploration phase as in Experiments 1 and 2. The participants were randomly assigned to only one of three conditions (between-participants design), in which visually-specified eye height: (1) matched the body-based eye height *(0 cm)*, (2) was 50 cm lower than body-based eye height (*−50 cm*, here the position of the head could not go lower than the bed surface in comparison to Experiment 2), or (3) was 50 cm higher than body-based eye height *(+50 cm)*. Participants completed 18 trials (4, 5 and 6 meters, each six times in a random blocked order). The procedure for reporting the distances was the same as in Experiments 1 and 2.

4.4.2 Results & Discussion

Due to technical errors with the HMD, the data of four participants were excluded from the analysis. I analyzed the verbal distance estimates using a repeated measures ANOVA with distance (4, 5, 6 m) and repetition (1–6) as within-subjects factors, eye height (−50, 0, or +50 cm) as a between-participants factor, and distance estimates as the dependent variable. As expected, distance was significant, with the estimates of distance increasing linearly with increasing distance, $F(2, 70) = 201.51, p < .001, \eta_p^2 = .85$.

The repeated measures ANOVA revealed that the eye height manipulation had a significant effect on the estimated distances in the −50 cm ($M = 5.25, SE = 0.41$), 0 cm ($M = 4.37, SE = 0.24$), and +50 cm ($M = 3.10, SE = 0.38$) eye height conditions, $F(2, 35) = 9.32, p = .001, \eta_p^2 = .35$, suggesting that the participants did not rely on their visual information to determine their eye height to judge the egocentric distances (see **Figure 4-7**). Post hoc pairwise comparisons using Bonferroni correction confirmed significant differences between the -50 and 0 cm eye height conditions, $p = .047$, and the −50 and +50 cm conditions, $p < .001$. However, there was no reliable difference between the +50 and 0 cm conditions, $p = .241$, which may have been due to the greater variability of estimates in the prone position. In addition, the predictions for the 0 cm and +50 cm conditions differ by a smaller amount than the predictions for the -50 cm and 0 cm conditions. As in the previous experiments, there was an interaction between eye height condition and distance, $F(4, 140) = 6.47, p < .001, \eta_p^2 = .27$, with the differences between the eye height conditions increasing as a function of distance, supporting the body-based eye height hypothesis.

In contrast to the postures used in Experiments 1 and 2, there were two different eye height possibilities for the prone position. The participants could use their physical standing eye height (i.e., distance from their eyes to their feet), because the lack of experience in such a posture, which would suggest the use of an internalized eye height [182] when uncertain about the posture. The other predictor is the actual distance from the participants' eyes to the floor while lying prone, suggesting the use of body-based information to ensure the necessary flexibility of perceived eye height to motor experiences. To investigate which eye height was used, I calculated the distances based on their standing and actual eye height (mean eye height during the experiment — acquired from the motion capture data from tracking the HMD) and found that actual body-based eye height had the best fit (linear regression with backward elimination), $\beta = .53, t(36) = 3.69, p = .001$. The predicted distances based on the model of eye height informed by body-based cues also explained a significant proportion of variance in the participants' distance estimates, $R^2 = .28, F(1, 36) = 13.64, p = .001$.

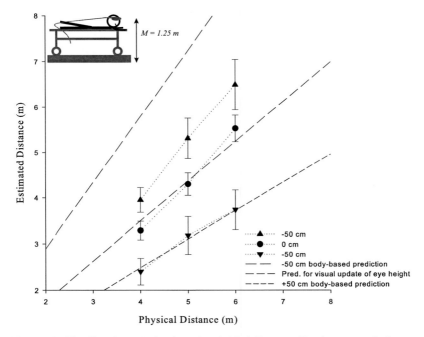

Figure 4-7: The effect of a manipulated visual eye height (−50 cm or +50 cm) on egocentric distances in a prone position on a bed (adjusted to be approximately at seated eye height) in comparison to the respective baseline condition (0 cm). Error bars represent ±1 SE. The actual mean participant eye height in the experiment is depicted in the left upper corner. **Note:** (a) The predictions are shifted by the observed underestimation in the baseline condition to account for the usually observed distance underestimation in head mounted displays (in an ideal world, the 0 cm estimates would correspond to the prediction, which is veridical performance). (b) If visually-specified eye height were used, there should be no differences and the prediction for visual eye height would apply for all conditions.

4.5 Experiment 4: The Reliability of Visual Information for Determining Eye Height in VR

It is valuable to investigate whether a lack of visual information, such as familiar size cues available in a rich-cue environment or incomplete stereo information due to the optics of the HMD and an accommodation-convergence mismatch (as was shown for a reaching paradigm in [13]), was the reason that participants relied on body-based information in the virtual environment. Thus, in the following experiment participants were required to rely on the visual information provided within two virtual environments (sparse and rich-cue) and were asked to directly estimate their virtual eye height in an adjustment task. If the visual information present in the virtual environments is sufficient to determine eye height, participants should be able to quite accurately adjust the virtual camera to match their actual eye height.

4.5.1 Method

Participants

Twenty-five paid (12 female) participants were recruited from the university community Tübingen, Germany. All had normal or corrected to normal visual acuity and were able to fuse stereo images. Age ranged from 21 to 47 years ($M = 28.0$).

Stimuli & Apparatus

I used the same technical setup and the same virtual environment (sparse-cue) as in Experiment 1-3 along with a second environment (rich-cue), which was a replica of a real office and provided a wealth of familiar size cues (chairs, tables, doors, etc.), see **Figure 4-8** . To control the virtual eye height, participants used a game pad to adjust the position of the camera in the y-axis.

Figure 4-8: Left: The sparse-cue environment used in the eye height adjustment task. **Right:** The rich-cue environment used for the eye height adjustment task.

Experimental Design & Procedure

All participants received written and verbal instructions and then the experimenter guided the participants to their standing position and helped them to don the HMD. Each environment included six training trials to familiarize the participants with the adjustment task where the participant adjusted the virtual camera's height to match their physical eye height. The camera either started 50 cm above or below their physical eye height in counterbalanced order. After the training trials, each participant completed 24 adjustment trials. When the participant finished one environment, the procedure was repeated with the second environment (counterbalanced, 48 trials in total).

4.5.2   Results & Discussion

For the analysis the adjustment trials were transformed into ratios by dividing the adjusted eye height by the real eye height of the corresponding participant. This means, a ratio of 1.0 reflects a perfect match between the visual virtual eye height and the real physical eye height of the participant. The data of one participant were removed from the analysis for being more than 3 SD above the mean.

I analyzed the eye height ratios using a repeated measures analysis of variance (ANOVA) with environment (sparse-cue and rich-cue) and repetition (24) as within-subjects factors and order as a between-participants variable, and the ratios as the dependent measure. There was no effect of order for the ratios, $p = 0.79$.

There was only a marginal effect of the environment, with the averaged ratios in the sparse-cue environment being overestimated ($M = 1.12, SE = 0.05$, standard errors denote between-participants errors) compared to the rich-cue environment ($M = 1.01, SE = 0.02$), $p = .064$. This suggests that if considering the group average, minimal visual information might already be sufficient to determine eye height (see **Figure 4-9**).

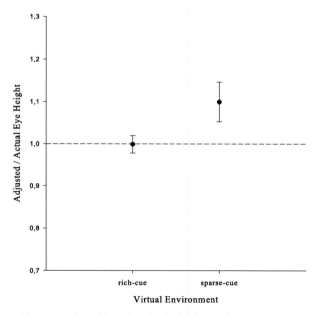

Figure 4-9: Mean ratio adjusted/actual eye height for the tested environments. Error bars represent ±1 SE.

In the rich-cue environment, the participants were veridical on average, and in the sparse environment, they were close to veridical in visually adjusting their virtual eye height to their corresponding physical eye height. These results suggest that on average, eye height could be approximately determined based on the available visual information in my experiments, suggesting that the obtained results might not be due to a lack of visual information for perceived eye height.

4.5.3 Considering the Error

Nevertheless, I observed quite some variability in the adjustment task, resulting in varying eye height judgments between participants, with a greater variability in the environment, where no cues, except HMD stereo and linear perspective, were present. In fact, when considering the absolute mean error in the visual eye height estimates in the rich-cue ($M = 13.24cm, SE = 2.09cm$) and sparse-cue ($M = 34.04cm, SE = 5.53cm$) environments, visually specified eye height might not be as veridical as assumed, suggesting that there is individual variability with regard to tendency to overestimate or underestimate visually adjusted eye height leading to a close to veridical average performance.

However, examples from the real world show that judging visually perceived eye height seems to be quite variable. For example, it has been shown that participants slightly underestimate their standing eye height, and drastically overestimate their eye height with respect to a lower ground plane when standing on an elevated ground plane of two meters height (see [182]). Similarly, real world experiments investigating the perceived eye level have shown that if humans judge their eye level, variability amounts to 1° visual angle, and the judgments are off by 2.2° of visual angle (e.g. [137]), even when the head is fixed and stable. In this specific task, the absolute error corresponds to 13.9 cm underestimation when judging eye level over a distance of 2.4 meters (c.f. [137]). Thus, I tentatively conclude that although individuals' estimates of their eye height in VEs were variable, the amount of this variability does not substantially differ from the variability reported in similar measures conducted in the real world. Indeed, this variability in individual assessments of visually perceived eye height in both real and virtual environments may provide a motivation for the perceptual system to take body-based information about eye height into account.

It is also necessary to consider that visually specified eye height can also change rapidly by a large degree, even if this change is not introduced along with a change in posture. These types of changes introduce yet another source of variability. For instance, consider a head movement for scanning the ground plane of an environment; this already alters the distance of the eyes to the ground by approximately 5 cm. Thus, visual perception of eye height might be quite variable (c.f. [182]), which could also be a reason why humans might rely on body-based cues to determine their eye height, at least in virtual environments.

4.6 Determining Eye Height and Distances in the Real World

While the results of Experiments 1-3 demonstrate a case of a reliance on body-based cues to determine eye height for perceiving egocentric distances if cues specifying eye height are in conflict, there is still the possibility that these findings are only specific to distance judgments in virtual environments. Although all participants had the possibility to look down and were encouraged to do so (where stereo cues should still be effective, see [38]), there is still an existing issue when using HMDs. One problem is that accommodation and convergence are decoupled and users are forced to accommodate to a constant distance (in the HMD accommodation distance is set to infinity) at which the virtual image of the displays appears (see [77, 13]).

To rule out that the observed effect occurs due to limitations of the VR technology used for Experiment 1-3, I conducted two additional real world studies to further investigate the observed effect in the virtual environments. Specifically, I sought for a solution to test both, the influence of experience and that of body-based cues on perceived distances in the real world when a correct accommodation and convergence coupling is available. In addition, I wanted to explore the accuracy of visually perceived eye height in the real world and how it compares to the results obtained in the VR setup.

4.7 Experiment 5: The Role of Body-based Eye Height versus Internalized Knowledge of Eye Height in the Real World

In Experiment 5 I attempt to investigate the role of internalized eye height based on experience in the real world. The results of Experiment 3 suggested that internalized eye height is likely not an important factor to determine eye height as hypothesized by other researchers (e.g. [182]). However, I used a quite uncommon posture (lying prone) to assess this in VR, and hence, also wanted to investigate this factor in a real world setting. In Experiment 5, I used a wooden ramp that participants were required to walk up while wearing a blindfold. When they were positioned on the top of the ramp, their lower body including the ramp was covered with a large textile to prevent participants from having visual access to the ramp height (while the view to the ground floor directly beneath the ramp was unobstructed).

Because participants received body-based information to eye height when they walked from the ground surface where the target objects were placed up to the ramp surface they were standing on when viewing the target, visual and body-based information to the ground surface was not decoupled. Due to walking up the ramp blindfolded, participants could also use their body-based cues to determine the height of the ramp to determine their eye height. Consequently, I would expect differences in the distance estimates if participants either rely on their internalized eye height (because the participants had no prior experience with an arbitrary ramp height) or rely on body-based cues with respect to the ramp surface. In contrast, if participants use the visual information to the ground surface or the body-based cues which indicate the new height with respect to the ground surface (i.e. by walking up the ramp) to determine their eye height, I would not expect a difference in the distance estimates.

4.7.1 Method

Participants

Twenty-nine (13 female) naïve observers participated in this experiment. Participants were recruited from the university community of Tübingen, Germany and were compensated for their participation at a rate of 8 €per hour. The age ranged from 20 to 47 years ($M = 27.52$). All participants had normal or corrected to normal vision.

Stimuli & Apparatus

The study was carried out in an empty free-walking space, 11.9 m × 11.7 m in size and 8 m high, with black walls and floor. Participants were either positioned directly on the floor in the free-walking space or on a wooden ramp with a podium height of 50 cm, a base length of 107 cm and a ramp length of 115 cm. The area of the podium was 50 cm × 50 cm. I used a black-painted safety goggle (Artec) which fits over glasses as a blindfold and noise canceling earphones (Stihl) to block out surrounding noise and the footstep sound when the experimenter was rearranging the target, while still enabling the participants to listen to the instructions when the experimenter was close. As target, I used an octagonal green paper disc with 21.5 cm radius. To cover the lower body including the feet (from solar plexus to the floor), a large black textile was used, which was wrapped around the participant and fixed with a belt.

Experimental Design & Procedure

Before the experiment started, the participants received written and oral instructions in a different room from where the experiment took place. When the participants indicated that they understood the task, participants were shown the same meter stick as in Experiment 1-3. The experimenter then guided the participants, who were blindfolded and donning the noise canceling earphones, into the room where the experiment took place. Participants were either positioned on (1) the floor where the targets were placed *(0 cm)* or (2) on a wooden ramp with a podium height of 50 cm *(+50 cm)*. All participants, regardless of condition were instructed not to move from this position; they were also instructed not to bend or lean about the waist during the trials. The black textile was then placed around participants to cover their lower body (and the wooden ramp in the corresponding condition, see **Figure 4-10**).

Once the setup was complete, the experimenter arranged the target for the first trial. After placing the target at the intended distance, the experimenter walked quietly behind the participants (at the same height, depending on condition, to avoid feedback due to talking to the participant from a different height) and indicated to participants that they could lower the blindfold and look at the target. The participants were instructed to estimate the distance to the middle of the target as accurately as possible in meters and centimeters. There were no time constraints for looking at the target; however, participants were instructed not to turn their head more than 90°, to prevent them from seeing the experimenter. Once participants were sure about the distance, they put back on the blindfold, turned their head 90° to the right and verbally reported the distance to the experimenter. Each participant completed 18 trials (4, 5 and 6 meters, each six times in a random blocked order). After completion of these trials, the experimenter asked the participants to verbally estimate their eye height with respect to the floor (with continuous vision) where the target was placed. The time needed for completing the whole experiment was approximately 45 minutes.

Figure 4-10: Left: Participant in the floor condition, wearing the noise canceling earphones and the blindfold, while the experimenter rearranged the target. **Right:** Participant in the ramp condition (50 cm high), wearing the noise canceling earphones and the blindfold until he receives the signal from the experimenter that he can lower the blindfold for judging the distance.

4.7.2 Results & Discussion

Distance estimates were analyzed using a repeated measures analysis of variance (ANOVA) with distance (4, 5, 6 m) and repetition (1-6) as within-subjects factors, eye height condition (0 cm, +50 cm) as the between subjects factor, and distance estimates as the dependent measure. As expected, distance was significant, with distance estimates increasing linearly across the 4 m to 5 m to 6 m distances, $F(2, 54) = 157.03, p < .001, \eta_p^2 = .85$.

The repeated measures ANOVA also revealed that in this experiment the manipulation of eye height had no effect on the estimated distances in the 0 cm ($M = 4.79, SE = 0.38$) and +50 cm ($M = 4.69, SE = 0.43$) eye height conditions, $p = .863$, suggesting that the participants did not use an internalized eye height or did not determine their eye height based on body-based information to the ramp surface. If this would have been the case, I would have expected that the distance estimates differ in the +50 cm and 0 cm condition, as the new height is unlikely to be internalized (or experienced) by the participants (see **Figure 4-11**). However, in this experiment the participants could have used both, the visual information indicating the distance to the ground floor, or body-based cues indicating the new height in relation to the ground floor, which were available from walking up the ramp blindfolded.

To investigate the reliability of visually specified eye height and to compare eye height judgments in the real world to the eye height adjustment task in VR (Experiment 4), the experimenter asked the participants to judge their eye height with respect to the ground surface where the target was placed. For analysis I transformed these judgments into ratios by dividing the estimated eye height by the real eye height of the corresponding participant. This means, a ratio of 1.0 reflects a perfect match between the estimated visual eye height and the real eye height of the participant with respect to the ground surface.

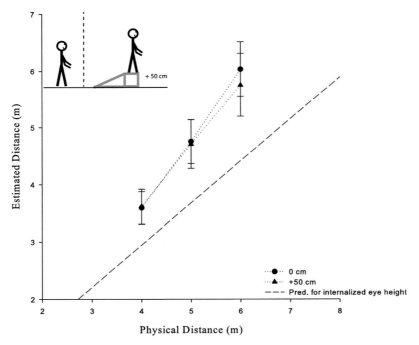

Figure 4-11: The effect of a changed visual eye height (+50 cm) on egocentric distances in a standing position on 50 cm high block in comparison to the respective baseline condition (0 cm). Error bars represent ±1 SE. If experience or an internalized eye height were used, there should be a difference in the estimates and the judgments in the +50 cm condition should align with the prediction based on an internalized eye height value.

I analyzed the eye height ratios using a univariate ANOVA with condition (0 cm and +50 cm) as a between-participants variable, and the ratios as the dependent measure. I found an effect of condition, $F(1, 27) = 4.25, p = .049, \eta_p^2 = .14$, with the ratios being larger in the +50 cm condition ($M = 1.09, SE = 0.05$) compared to the 0 cm condition ($M = 0.98, SE = 0.01$). These results suggest that visually perceived eye height is quite veridical on average in the real world, thus visual information seems to be sufficient to inform eye height. Of course, in the condition in which participants were standing on the floor, they only had to report a few centimeters below their height, so I would expect participants to be veridical in this condition because most people know their own height. However, considering the variability in the +50 cm condition, it was surprising to find a similar variability compared to that observed in experiment 4. In fact, when considering the absolute mean error in the visual eye height estimates in the 0 cm ($M = 3.93cm, SE = 1.20cm$) and +50 cm ($M = 31.27cm, SE = 7.81cm$) conditions, it seems that while these eye height judgments are veridical in the mean, they vary largely between individuals. These results correspond very closely to the findings in Experiment 4, where I found a similar variability in the eye height judgments based on visual information (see **Figure 4-12**).

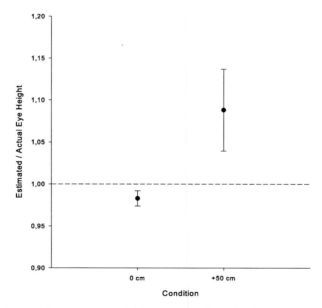

Figure 4-12: Verbal judgments of visual eye height in the real world with respect to the ground plane in the 0cm (floor) or +50cm (ramp) condition. Error bars represent ±1 SE.

Interestingly, participants' estimates of distance *did not differ* even though their individual perceptions of their visual eye height were less accurate in the +50 cm condition. In addition, the variability in the distance estimates between the 0 cm and +50 cm condition was roughly the same. Thus, the on average close to veridical judgments of visually perceived eye height and the similarity in the distance judgments suggest that body-based cues and/or visual information could be used to determine eye height. Consequently, I sought for a solution to decouple visual and body-based information specifying eye height in the real world.

4.8 Experiment 6: Usage of Body-Based Eye Height with a Shifted Frame of Reference in the Real World

To find a solution for this problem and to be able to provide the participants with an elevated ground surface which corresponds to that in Experiment 5, I introduce a frame of reference shift in the real world, which allows us to investigate body-based cues and visual information separately for determining eye height in the real world. To achieve this, I put participants on their backs and asked them to judge distances on a high wall, either with their feet directly against the wall (0 cm), or against a cube with a height of 50 centimeters (+50 cm). In both cases the participants' lower body and the cube was covered by a large non see-through textile.

By using such a setup, the participants could use the visual information to assess their eye height with respect to the wall. If this is the case I would expect no difference in the distance judgments between the 0 cm and +50 cm conditions, because the relation between the judged eye height and the corresponding angle of declination should remain invariant. However, if humans primarily rely on body-based cues to determine their eye height, I would expect differences similar to what I observed in Experiments 1-3, because the participants did not gain body-based information to the new "height" with respect to the "floor" where the target was placed, in contrast to Experiment 5.

4.8.1 Method

Participants

Twenty-six (12 female) participants were recruited from the university community Tübingen, Germany and were compensated for their time at a rate of 8 €per hour. All had normal or corrected to normal visual acuity. The age ranged from 18 to 52 years ($M = 29.40$). None of the participants was aware of the purpose of the experiment.

Stimuli & Apparatus

The study was carried out in a large, almost empty hall, 23.70 m × 11.70 m in size and 10 m high, with black walls and floor. Approximately in the middle of the hall, I set up poster boards, which were covered with black textiles to prevent the participants from seeing specific familiar size cues in the hall (e.g. doors). Between the poster boards was cushion material on the floor to enable the participants to lie comfortably on the cushion on their back. Directly on the wall I placed a cube (50 cm × 50 cm × 50 cm), which had only one solid surface (custom made).

I used a black-painted safety goggle (Artec) which fits over glasses as a blindfold and noise canceling earphones (Stihl) to block out surrounding noise and the sound when the experimenter was rearranging the target, while still enabling the participants to listen to the instructions of the experimenter. I used black non see-through textiles to cover the cube and the lying participant's lower body. As target, I used the same octagonal green paper disc with 21.5 cm radius as in Experiment 5. The target was connected with a transparent fishing line and hung up at approximately 8 m height, so it could be adjusted by the experimenter to the different target distances. The experimenter sat behind the poster boards outside of the view of the participant. The fishing line was not visible from a distance.

Experimental Design & Procedure

Before the experiment started, the participants received written and oral instructions in a different room than where the experiment took place. When the participant indicated that s/he understood everything, the participant was shown the same meter stick as in the other experiments. The experimenter then guided the participant blindfolded and equipped with the noise canceling earphones into the hall where the experiment took place. The experimenter guided the participant to the cushion, which was positioned between two poster boards, and helped them to lie down, putting their feet against the wall through the cube *(0 cm)*, or against the solid surface of the cube *(+50 cm)*, depending on the condition. The participant was then equipped with a black textile to cover the cube and the lower body of the participant, while still enabling an unobstructed view to the ground surface (wall) where the target was placed.

Once the setup was complete, the experimenter walked behind the poster boards and arranged the target for the first trial by moving the fishing line. After placing the target at the intended distance, the experimenter indicated to the participant that s/he should lower the blindfold and look at the target. The participants were instructed to estimate the distance to the middle of the target as accurate as possible in meters and centimeters. There were no time constraints for looking at the target. Once the participant was sure about the distance, he put back on the blindfold, turned his head 90° to the left and verbally reported the distance to the experimenter. Each participant completed 18 trials (4, 5 and 6 meters, each six times in a random blocked order). After the trials, the experimenter asked the participants to verbally estimate their eye height with respect to the "ground" (in this case the wall, with continuous vision) where the target was placed. The time needed for completing the whole experiment was approximately 45 minutes.

4.8.2 Results & Discussion

Due to technical difficulties, the data of one participant were excluded from the analysis. I analyzed the verbal distance estimates using a repeated measures ANOVA with distance (4, 5, 6 m) and repetition (1–6) as within-subjects factors, eye height (0 or +50 cm) as a between-participants factor, and distance estimates as the dependent variable. As expected, distance was significant, with the estimates of distance increasing linearly with increasing distance, $F(2, 46) = 91.44, p < .001, \eta_p^2 = .80$.

The repeated measures ANOVA revealed that the eye height manipulation had a significant effect on the estimated distances in the 0 cm $(M = 6.85, SE = 0.55)$, and +50 cm $(M = 5.15, SE = 0.53)$ eye height conditions, $F(2, 23) = 4.96, p = .036, \eta_p^2 = .18$, suggesting that the participants did not rely on their visual information to determine their eye height to judge the egocentric distances (see **Figure 4-13**). Surprisingly, the participants were overestimating the distance in the baseline condition, a fact likely associated with the shifted frame of reference with respect to gravity, which needs further investigation.

As in Experiments 1-3, I also found an interaction between eye height condition and distance, $F(2, 46) = 6.10, p = .004, \eta_p^2 = .21$, with the differences between the eye height conditions increasing as a function of distance, as would be predicted by the body-based eye height hypothesis.

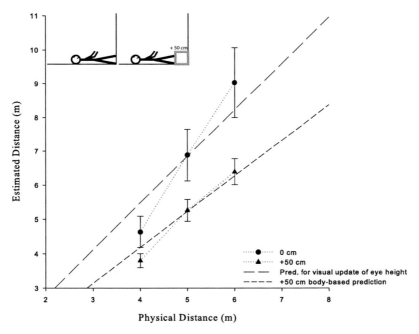

Figure 4-13: The effect of a changed visual eye height (+50 cm) on egocentric distances in a lying position with feet against a hidden 50 cm block in comparison to the respective baseline condition (feet against wall - 0 cm). Error bars represent ±1 SE. If visually-specified eye height were used, there should be no differences and the prediction for visual eye height would apply for the +50 cm condition.

In addition to the distance judgments, I analyzed again the eye height estimates in the real world. For analysis I transformed these judgments into ratios by dividing the estimated eye height by the real eye height of the corresponding participant.

I analyzed the eye height ratios using a univariate ANOVA with condition (0 cm and +50 cm) as a between-participants variable, and the ratios as the dependent measure. I found no effect of condition, p = .341, with the ratios being not reliably different in the +50 cm condition ($M = 1.06, SE = 0.05$) from the 0 cm condition ($M = 1.00, SE = 0.03$) (see **Figure 4-14**).

These results confirm the previous findings that even in the real world, visually perceived eye height is quite veridical on average, but variable. In fact, when considering the absolute errors in the visual eye height estimates in the 0 cm ($M = 13.25cm, SE = 2.06cm$) and +50 cm ($M = 31.69cm, SE = 8.24cm$) conditions, the variability was again very similar compared to Experiment 4 and 5.

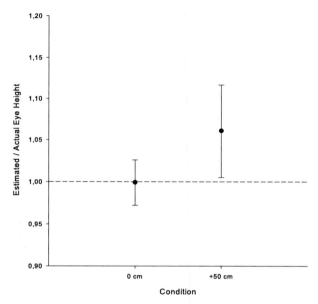

Figure 4-14: Verbal judgments of visual eye height in the real world with respect to the ground plane in the 0cm (wall) or +50cm (cube) condition. Error bars represent ±1 SE.

However, there is still the possibility that the participants used their misperceived visually specified eye height to judge the egocentric distances, therefore I calculated the predicted distances based on both, the visually perceived (judged) eye height and the body-based eye height (the physical eye height from eyes to the feet). Using a linear regression with backward elimination I found that the predictions using body-based eye height has the best fit, $\beta = .42, t(23) = 3.62, p = .035$. The predicted distances based on the model of body-based eye height informed by body-based cues also explained a significant proportion of variance in the participants' distance estimates, $R^2 = .18, F(1, 36) = 5.02, p = .035$, while the predictions based on the misperceived eye height based on visual information could not reliably predict the observed distance judgments, $p = .645$. Thus, these results suggest that body-based cues are also important in the real world, where accommodation and convergence cues are correct and available. In combination, Experiments 5 and 6 provide additional evidence that there are cases where humans rely more on body-based cues for determining eye height not only in virtual environments but also in the real world and that experience/internalized eye height is likely not used to determine eye height as hypothesized by others (see [182]).

4.9   Summary & Discussion

With this set of studies, I demonstrate that there are cases where humans rely on body-based cues to determine eye height for the scaling of distances. In contrast to the theory stating that visual information is dominant over information from other sensory modalities (e.g. [158]), my results demonstrate a case where body-based cues are used to determine eye height, even when visual information to inform eye height was available, albeit quite variable (Experiment 4, 5 and 6). Moreover, the real world results support the results which I obtained using virtual reality technology, suggesting that the found effect on distance judgments is not due to limitations of the used technology, namely an accommodation-convergence mismatch in a HMD. While there is compelling evidence that an accommodation-convergence mismatch has effects on perceived distance (at least in reaching space, see [13, 77]), it is unlikely that this fully accounts for the strength of the observed effects in action space. Furthermore, the effect of such a mismatch is usually that convergence is pulled towards the accommodation distance (c.f. [13]). The used HMD in Experiments 1-4 features collimated optics, which simulate an accommodation distance at infinity. Thus, the convergence should be pulled towards infinity, which should result in overestimation as observed in Bingham and colleagues elegant work [13]. Thus, all conditions should be similarly affected by such a mismatch, because if eye height would be reliant for example on stereo information, it should be overestimated by a similar amount across all conditions. Thus, the observed reliance on body-based cues to determine eye height might be a general phenomenon rather than specific to virtual environments.

Interestingly, the results also suggest that determining eye height from body based-cues can occur without the need for perceptual-locomotor feedback (see especially Experiment 5). This is similar to findings from other eye height related studies, where no direct perceptual-motor feedback was provided but where, for example, immediate effects of a false or elevated floor on perceived size were observed (see [225, 182]). However, related work suggests that providing feedback in action space can be important to provide the opportunity to calibrate actions to altered visual cues (see for example [162, 129]), specifically in a HMD. Additionally, recent research in near space suggests that a calibration of eye height to a new support surface (e.g. a table) is necessary for veridical reaching performance (see e.g. [31, 139]). Thus, in both, action and reaching space recalibration methodologies (like in [139, 31, 162]), more experiments could be conducted to specifically investigate the calibration of actions based on perceptual-motor feedback to a decoupled visual and body-based information about eye height to the ground plane in action space.

The results also suggest that even though there are cases where humans rely more on body-based cues to determine their eye height, it is combined with the angle of declination below the horizon to perceive distances, suggesting that the angle of declination is a robust source of information [178, 179, 137]. But why do observers then combine body-based cues (eye height) and visual information (angle of declination) instead of fully relying on visual information? Throughout my experiments, I observed that visually-specified eye height is on average judged veridical, however, I also observed quite some individual variability. One might argue that the experiments did not provide sufficient information for determining eye height, which is understandable, especially considering the presented limitations in VR. However, the real world experiments (where eye height is also on average judged veridical) were conducted in full-cue environments with a maximum "manipulated" eye height of 1.95m – 2.20m, where even stereo information (accommodation & convergence) is still informative (see [38]). Thus, it seems that visual information may not be as reliable in general to determine eye height, and consequently, it would make sense to rely more on body-based cues for determining eye height and to combine this information with other reliable information (visual information for the angle of declination).

Thus, the results also indicate, that while the eye height unit is mainly informed by body-based cues and the angle of declination provided by vision (e.g. [137]), both are consistently used in combination across different postures to ensure perceptual constancy in ecologically valid contexts. Such a mechanism allows individuals to perceive an unchanging surrounding environment. However, more research is necessary to fully understand how this body-based information is used to determine eye height. With the used experimental design, it is not possible to fully disentangle what I describe as body-based cues, which likely include but are not limited to proprioceptive, haptic and/or vestibular cues. In addition, one possibility is that all available cues for determining eye height from various modalities, including vision, are integrated along a Bayesian multi-sensory integration approach, where cues are weighted with respect to their reliability across the various contexts. In my experimental context, it could be that cues to eye height from other modalities were weighted higher than the visual cues specifying eye height; thereby leading to the observed influences on perceived distance (e.g. see [22] for such an approach). Yet, there are possibly other contexts in which visual cues to eye height are weighted higher than information specifying eye height from other modalities. Additional studies need to be conducted to determine if this is occurring for the perception of eye height.

Nevertheless, these findings are surprising for several reasons. Prior to my experiments, the sensory modality used to specify eye height had not yet been empirically investigated (at least for eye height to the ground surface), despite the popular assumption that the information used to determine eye height would come largely from the visual modality [158]. My results suggest, that in some contexts, individuals use body-based cues to determine eye height for distance perception. These contexts are not limited to virtual environments, but can also occur in the real world. It is important to note that this is a surprising finding, even if it would be only in virtual environments, as previous literature has hypothesized that eye height is either stored as internalized knowledge or determined by visual information alone. My results provide indicate that this is not always the case.

Overall, these results highlight the importance of body-based cues in visual perception [123, 155, 107] and demonstrate that in an environment with a regular ground surface [227] the body may contribute important information for a visual task i.e. distance perception. This is also consistent with and extends previous literature stating that eye height is an important source of information for perceiving different aspects of the spatial layout of our environment [41, 224, 225]. Most importantly, the present work reveals, that even in a task which does not involve locomotion (e.g., [23, 22]) or navigation (e.g., [206]), body-based cues are important for the perception of the spatial layout of our environment. Throughout the conducted studies, body-based cues appear to be used to determine eye height for the estimation of distances.

Chapter 5

Eye Height Manipulations to Improve Distance Perception in Virtual Reality

5.1 Introduction

The results from the series of experiments presented in the previous chapter suggest that humans rely more on their body-based cues to inform their eye height when visual and body-based sources of information specifying eye height are in conflict. Thus, manipulations of the virtual eye height within an IVE should have predictable consequences on perceived distances in IVEs. Motivated by the previous findings, I propose a possible solution to reduce distance underestimation in IVEs, which is not dependent on prior interaction within the IVE and has similar effects on both, an action-based and a cognitive measure. Specifically, by manipulating virtual eye height, I might be able to reduce distance underestimation in IVEs without distorting the majority of the cues to distance perception or requiring additional expensive equipment and expertise. In addition, the proposed idea could be applied to address and reduce individual underestimation, as distance underestimation strongly varies between different people. Furthermore, the experiments in Chapter 4 have already shown that a conflict in the sensory information specifying eye height can influence common measures of perceived distance including verbal reports (in contrast to minification, see [230]) and is, as such, a promising candidate to counter the distance underestimation in a similar way across different measures. In the following, I describe why eye height manipulations might be an easy and effective tool to correct and/or change the perceived spatial layout of virtual environments.

With my prior findings, it is conceivable that the relationship between eye height and perceived egocentric distance can be exploited to reduce individual distance underestimation by using a simple virtual eye height manipulation. However, the degree of the virtual eye height manipulation required to reduce or even eliminate distance underestimation is not yet known. If the individual underestimation of a person is known and assuming that humans primarily rely on their body-based cues to inform eye height in the context of VR, there are in principle two approaches to determine the required manipulation. Consider a small numerical example:

An observer with a physical eye height of 1.65 meters sees a target at 5 meters distance in a HMD-based virtual environment. According to the relationship between eye height and the angle of declination, the corresponding angle of declination is $EH/d = 1.65/5 = tan^{-1}(0.33)$. Now assume the observer reports 4 meters instead of 5 meters due to the distance underestimation effect which is often reported to be on average about 20% in HMDs (see [160]). To reduce this distance underestimation I can lower the virtual eye height, such that the displayed distance is perceived as 20% (or 1 meter) further away. To calculate the eye height manipulation necessary to shift the perceived distance by 20%, I can determine the angle of declination for a distance, which would be 20% further away than the real target, in this case 6 meters, where the angle of declination would be $EH/d = 1.65/6 = tan^{-1}(0.275)$. Due to the relationship between eye height, the angle of declination and perceived distance, I can now calculate the eye height manipulation necessary to compensate for the 20% distance underestimation, $tan^{-1}(0.275) \times 5 = 1.375$. Hence, by lowering the virtual eye height by 27.5 centimeters, the observer should perceive the indicated distance (5 m) close to veridical (this example is what I refer to as linear prediction).

However, this approach does not consider that distance underestimation might also apply to the *extended* distances. In the given example, the 1 meter distance required to achieve veridical performance will likely also be affected by the 20% underestimation, thus will only be perceived as 80 centimeters. Using a (what I refer to as multiplicative) variant which tries to account for this, the above example changes according to the following: Consider the same example as described above with an observer with a physical eye height of 1.65 meters sees a target at 5 meters distance in a HMD-based virtual environment. If he judges 4 meters instead of 5 meters, the amount required to counter this underestimation is not only 1 meter (because this will also be underestimated by 20%) but 1.25 meters. Thus, the required hypothetical distance will be 6.25 meters, which results in the corresponding angle of declination, $EH/d = 1.65/6.25 = tan^{-1}(0.264)$. This means, the required eye height manipulation will be $tan^{-1}(0.264) \times 5 = 1.32$. Hence by lowering the eye height by 33 centimeters, distances should be judged close to veridical. Nevertheless, this approach may pose some problems. As already can be seen by assuming only 20% underestimation the required eye height manipulation is already 5.5 centimeters more compared to the first approach. Thus, in cases where participants underestimate by 50% the required manipulation will be quite large and likely noticed by the observer. Furthermore, distance underestimation varies not only between individuals, but can also vary within individuals, even within different distances. Thus, taking the prior underestimation into account might not guarantee veridical results. Therefore, in the present work I tested both approaches to investigate which one is more suitable for achieving the goal of reducing or even countering distance underestimation in IVEs. **Figure 5-1** illustrates how a manipulated eye height of an observer (with an actual eye height of 1.65 meters) should change the perceived distance (for a target at 5 meters) for different amounts of underestimation based on the relationship depicted in section 3.1.2 and the assumption that eye height is informed primarily by body-based cues.

If the relationship depicted in **Figure 5-1** is true, I should be able to selectively alter perceived distances in IVEs for individual observers, which would make eye height a valuable tool

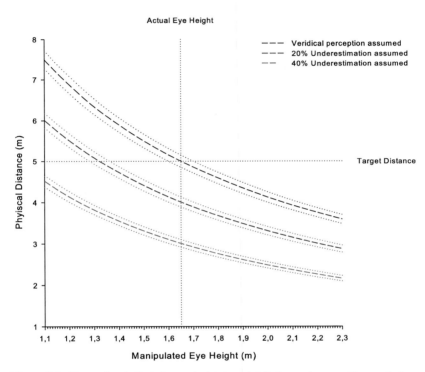

Figure 5-1: The predicted effect of a manipulated eye height for an observer with an actual eye height of 1.65 meters and a target at 5 meters distance. Important to note are the differences in slope between the depicted scenarios and the asymmetry (a raise in the virtual eye height will have less of an effect than lowering the eye height). The dotted lines above and below the plotted functions indicate a change of ±5 centimeters in eye height and how this already can change perceived distances.

to reduce or even eliminate distance underestimation in IVEs. However, I also seek for a solution that is usable across different measures of distance. For example, it has been shown recently that verbal reports and direct blind-walking as response measures are affected differently by minification [230], which might limit the usability of this approach to generate a close to veridical perception of distances in IVEs depending on the application, for example in collaborative scenarios where IVEs might be explored differently. Thus, I first investigated whether an eye height manipulation influences egocentric distances when measured with direct blind-walking, which is the most commonly used action-based measure for assessing egocentric distances (see [160]). In contrast to minification, where verbal estimates are not affected by minification and blind-walking is strongly affected by it, the presented set of experiments in Chapter 4 provides evidence that verbal reports of distance are affected in accord with my prediction by an eye height manipulation. However, there is still the possibility that the influence of a manipulated eye height on verbal estimates was occurring due to cognitive influences. Thus, I first conducted an experiment using the same generic eye height manipulation as in Experiment 1 to investigate whether there is a similar pattern on perceived distances measured with direct blind-walking as previously observed for verbal reports.

5.2 Experiment 7: The Influence of a Manipulated Eye Height on an Action-Based Measure

In this first experiment in this series, I sought to replicate the previously obtained results, which show that eye height is informed by body-based cues. To test whether to influence of eye height is consistent across different measures (in contrast to minification, see e.g. [230]), I used the same design as in Experiment 1 but employed an action-based measure to assess perceived egocentric distances. In addition, I used two different environments, one sparse- and one rich-cue environment to investigate whether the eye height manipulation has the same predicted effects on perceived distances in a realistic replica environment of an office space.

5.2.1 Method

Participants

Thirty-nine (18 female) participants were recruited from the university community of Tübingen, Germany, and were compensated for their time at a rate of 8 € per hour. All had normal or corrected to normal visual acuity and were screened for the ability to fuse stereo displays. The age ranged from 18 to 65 years ($M = 26.44$).

Stimuli & Apparatus

The study was carried out in a fully-tracked free-walking space, 11.9 m × 11.7 m × 8 m high, with black walls and a black floor. I used two virtual environments: one consisted of a flat ground plane without any familiar size cues (sparse-cue environment) and the other was a replica of a real-world office (rich-cue environment), including familiar size cues (e.g. chairs, tables and doors), shadows and realistic light mapping. The sparse-cue environment included a visual horizon and a blue sky/background and the ground plane was textured with a random stone pattern to eliminate texture gradient depth cues while conserving linear perspective cues. To provide a correct implicit and explicit horizon, a software correction was implemented to compensate for radial distortion due to the optics of the used HMD (if uncorrected, the horizon or walls in the office would appear as a curve at the outer regions of the optics). The judged distances were indicated by a target that was modeled as an octagonal green disc with a radius of 21.5 cm and a height of 1.4 cm.

Participants saw the virtual environments through an Nvis nVisor SX60 HMD (Nvis Inc., Reston, VA, USA) with a resolution of 1280 × 1024 pixels per eye (in stereo). The HMD has a refresh rate of 60 Hz per eye and a contrast of 100:1. The field of view of the SX60 is 60° diagonal, with a spatial resolution of approximately 2.2 arc-minutes per pixel. The position and orientation of the HMD was tracked by a 16-camera Vicon MX13 (Vicon, Oxford, UK) tracking system. The average end-to-end latency of this network (i.e., tracking the HMD, processing the captured data, and updating the view in the virtual environment accordingly) was measured using photodiodes with the method proposed by Di Luca [40] and was approximately 40.8 ms $(SD = 24.0ms)$.

Experimental Design & Procedure

All participants started the experiment by completing a written consent form, which was approved by the ethical committee of the University of Tübingen, Germany. The participants received written and verbal instructions.

The experiment started with a short training phase in the real world to familiarize the participants with the blind walking task, where they had to walk blindfolded to self-chosen landmarks on the floor and were guided back by the experimenter without receiving feedback about their walked training distance. After the training, the participants started with a five minute exploration phase to familiarize them with the virtual environment. The participants were randomly assigned to one of three conditions, in which visually-specified EH: (1) matched the body-based EH *(0 cm)*; (2) was 50 cm lowered *(-50 cm)*; or (3) was 50 cm raised *(+50 cm)*. During the exploration phase, the participants were instructed to stand comfortably upright. They were not allowed to turn, bend, or lean forward or to the sides, nor were they allowed to take any step away from the standing position.

After the exploration phase, the distance estimation phase started. The target was displayed at a certain distance, and the participants had as much time as they needed to get an impression of the target distance. When the participants indicated they were ready, the screen of the HMD was blanked; then the participants closed their eyes, walked towards the target and stopped where they believed the target to be, see **Figure 5-2**. After walking to the target, the participants remained blindfolded and were guided back to the starting point on a random curvy path through the tracking space. Thus, the participants received no feedback about their walked distance. When the participants were positioned on a predefined location, the next target was displayed after the participants indicated their readiness.

Figure 5-2: Participant blind-walking to a virtual target. During this and the following Experiments, the NVisor SX 60 HMD and the custom built tracking belt, the participant is wearing around his waist, were used.

Every participant completed 18 trials (4, 5 and 6 m, each six times in a random blocked order). After completion of the blind-walking task in the first environment and a five minute break, the participants repeated the task in the second environment (36 trials in total). The order of the environments was counterbalanced. After finishing the task in both environments, the experimenter helped the participants to take off the equipment and asked them to complete a short questionnaire.

5.2.2   Results & Discussion

One participant was removed from the analysis, because in one of the first trials he attempted to walk further than the boundaries of the tracking space. I conducted a repeated measures analysis of variance (ANOVA) with environment (sparse-cue and rich-cue), distance (4, 5 and 6 m) and repetition (1-6) as within-subjects factors, EH (-50, 0, or +50 cm) and environment order as between-participants variables, and distance estimates as the dependent measure. As expected, distance was significant, with the estimates of distance increasing linearly from the 4 to 5 to 6 m distances, $F(2, 64) = 594.44, p < .001, \eta_p^2 = .95$.

In addition, the walked distances differed between the rich-cue and sparse-cue environment, $F(1, 32) = 62.85, p < .001, \eta_p^2 = .66$, with the walked distances being greater in the rich-cue environment ($M = 3.70m, SE = 0.20$) compared to the sparse-cue environment ($M = 3.29m, SE = 0.22$), regardless of order in which the environments were presented, $p = .925$ (see **Figure 5-3**).

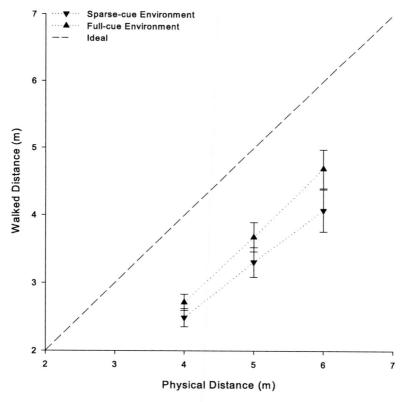

Figure 5-3: Baseline (0 cm) performances in the sparse- and rich-cue environment, where the participants walked significantly further in the rich-cue environment. Error bars represent ±1 SE.

As predicted, the eye height manipulation had a strong effect on the walked distances, $F(2, 32) = 21.25, p < .001, \eta_p^2 = .57$. In addition, there was an interaction between EH condition and distance, $F(4, 160) = 11.77, p < .001, \eta_p^2 = .42$, with the differences between the EH conditions increasing as a function of increase in distance, which is predicted by the body-based EH hypothesis. Furthermore, I found an interaction between the environment and eye height conditions, $F(2, 32) = 7.84, p = .002, \eta_p^2 = .33$, which indicates that the eye height manipulation influenced the perceived distances differently, depending on the environment. For further analyses of the results, I analyzed the walked distances separately for each used environment.

Rich-cue environment: I analyzed the walked distances in the rich-cue environment using a repeated measures ANOVA with distance (4, 5, 6 m) and repetition (1-6) as within-subjects factors, EH (-50, 0, or +50 cm) as a between-participants factor, and distance estimates as the dependent measure. As expected, distance was significant, with the estimates of distance increasing linearly from the 4 to 5 to 6 m distances, $F(2, 70) = 490.64, p < .001, \eta_p^2 = .93$.

In addition, the eye height manipulation had a significant effect on the estimated distances in the -50 cm ($M = 5.35m, SE = 0.24$), 0 cm ($M = 3.70m, SE = 0.20$), and +50 cm ($M = 3.41m, SE = 0.18$) eye height conditions, $F(2, 35) = 25.63, p < .001, \eta_p^2 = .59$, indicating that if there is a discrepancy, humans rely on body-based eye height rather than visually-specified eye height to determine egocentric distances using an action-based measure (see **Figure 5-4**).

Post-hoc comparisons using Fisher's LSD confirmed significant differences between the -50 and 0 cm eye height conditions, $p < .001$ and the -50 and +50 cm conditions, $p < .001$. However, in this case the prediction for the walked distances in the 0 and +50 cm conditions differed only by a small amount, which is also reflected by a non-significant difference between those conditions, $p = .347$. In addition, there was an interaction between eye height condition and distance, $F(4, 160) = 9.97, p < .001, \eta_p^2 = .36$, with the differences between the eye height conditions increasing as a function of increases in distance, as would be predicted by the body-based eye height hypothesis.

To test my prediction regarding body-based eye height, I predicted the walked distances based on my model (see **Figure 2**). A linear regression confirmed the body-based eye height hypothesis, as the calculated distances based on body-based eye height significantly predicted the actual walked distances, $\beta = .724, t(37) = 6.29, p < .001$. The predicted distances also explained a significant proportion of variance in the participants' distance estimates, $R^2 = .524, F(1, 37) = 39.60, p < .001$.

Sparse-cue environment: Similar to the rich-cue environment, I analyzed the walked distances in the sparse-cue environment using a repeated measures ANOVA with distance (4, 5, 6 m) and repetition (1-6) as within-subjects factors, EH (-50, 0, or +50 cm) as a between-participants factor, and distance estimates as the dependent measure. As expected, distance was significant, with the estimates of distance increasing linearly from the 4 to 5 to 6 m distances, $F(2, 70) = 382.07, p < .001, \eta_p^2 = .92$. The eye height manipulation in the sparse-cue environment had a significant effect on the walked distances in the -50 cm ($M = 4.17m, SE = 0.20$),

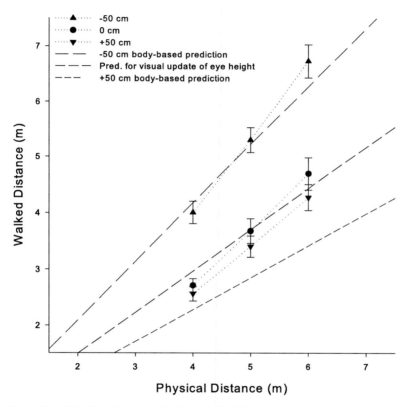

Figure 5-4: The effect of a manipulated visual EH (-50 cm or +50 cm) on egocentric distances in comparison to the respective baseline condition (0 cm) assessed with blind-walking in a rich-cue environment. Error bars represent ±1 SE.

0 cm ($M = 3.29m, SE = 0.22$), and +50 cm ($M = 2.90m, SE = 0.18$) eye height conditions, $F(2, 35) = 11.16, p < .001, \eta_p^2 = .39$, indicating that also in an environment without any familiar size cues, humans rely on body-based eye height rather than visually-specified eye height to determine distances when assessed with an action-based measure (see **Figure 5-5**).

Post-hoc comparisons using Fisher's LSD confirmed significant differences between the -50 and 0 cm eye height conditions, $p = .003$ and the -50 and +50 cm conditions, $p < .001$. However, similar to the rich-cue environment, the prediction for the walked distances in the 0 and +50 cm conditions differ only by a marginal amount, thus I did not find a significant difference between the 0 cm and +50 cm conditions, $p = .174$. In addition, I again found an interaction between eye height condition and distance, $F(4, 160) = 6.37, p < .001, \eta_p^2 = .27$, with the differences between the eye height conditions increasing as a function of increases in distance, supporting the notion that body-based eye height is used (see **Figure 5-5**).

To test again my prediction regarding body-based eye height, I predicted the walked distances based on the model (see **Figure 2**). A linear regression confirmed the hypothesis, as the calculated distances based on body-based eye height significantly predicted the actual walked distances, $\beta = .627, t(37) = 4.82, p < .001$. The predicted distances also explained a significant proportion of variance in the participants' distance estimates, $R^2 = .393, F(1, 37) = 23.26, p < .001$.

The results suggest that a manipulation of the visually-specified (virtual) eye height by ±50 cm has similar effects on an action-based measure compared to verbal reports. This means, the underestimation or expansion of perceived distances due to an eye height manipulation compared to the baseline seems not to be different for the two most commonly used measures of perceived egocentric distances. Thus, using an eye height manipulation to selectively counter distance underestimation should result in an increase in the perceived distances also if assessed with an action-based measure.

5.3 Experiment 8: Manipulating Eye Height to Reduce Distance Underestimation

To investigate whether I can use eye height manipulations to reduce distance underestimation in IVEs, I conducted an experiment, where I assessed the individual underestimation of the participants and measured them again after a short break with a manipulated eye height (using the linear approach described in the introduction), to observe whether they walk closer towards the intended distance. If the predictions hold true, participants should walk considerably closer to the intended distance with a manipulated eye height compared to the previous session when they experienced the environment with an unaltered virtual eye height.

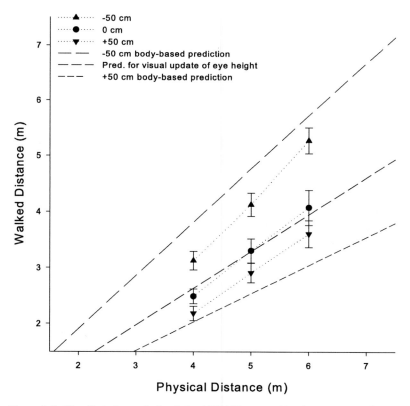

Figure 5-5: The effect of a manipulated visual EH (-50 cm or +50 cm) on egocentric distances in comparison to the respective baseline condition (0 cm) assessed with blind-walking in a sparse-cue environment. Error bars represent ±1 SE.

5.3.1 Method

Participants

Twenty-four (9 female) participants were recruited from the university community of Tübingen, Germany, and were compensated for their time at a rate of 8 € per hour. All had normal or corrected to normal visual acuity and were screened for the ability to fuse stereo displays. The age ranged from 18 to 52 years ($M = 26.29$).

Stimuli & Apparatus

For this experiment, I used the same technical setup as in Experiment 7 with the difference that I only used the sparse-cue virtual environment for this experiment. I chose the sparse-cue environment because distance seemed more underestimated in Experiment 7 compared to the rich-cue environment. Thus, I assumed it would be easier to detect an effect of a manipulated eye height, because there is more room for potential improvement.

Experimental Design & Procedure

All participants started the experiment by completing a written consent form, which was approved by the ethical committee of the University of Tübingen, Germany. The participants received written and verbal instructions.

The experiment started with the same training phase as in Experiment 7 to familiarize the participants with the blind walking task. The main part of the experiment consisted of two sessions: In the first, I measured the individual distance estimation with the blind walking task. In the second session, participants were randomly assigned to either repeating the same task (control) or experiencing a manipulated eye height to compensate for their distance underestimation in the first session (eye height manipulation). The manipulated eye height was calculated automatically fusing the results in session one, based on the linear model described in the introduction of this chapter (see also **Figure 3-3** in Chapter 3). Both groups of participants started both sessions with a 30 second exploration phase to familiarize them with the environment and technical setup. Subsequently the blind walking task started, where they were instructed to walk blindfolded purposefully and decisively to the indicated target using the same procedure as in Experiment 7.

Every participant completed 36 blind-walking trials in total (3, 4, 5, 6, 7 and 8 meters, each three times in a random blocked order per session). After completion of the blind walking task in the first session and a five-minute break, the participants repeated the task in the second session. After finishing the task in both sessions, the experimenter helped the participants to take off the equipment and asked them to complete a questionnaire.

5.3.2 Results & Discussion

To analyze the results of Experiment 8, I created ratios for the walked distances in each session by dividing the mean walked distance by the mean actual distance. To assess the effect of the manipulated eye height for the manipulated eye height group and a potential training effect in the control group, I created a difference score by subtracting the mean ratio of session one from the mean ratio of session two. Thus, a positive difference score indicates that the participants walked further in session two compared to session one, while a negative difference score indicates the opposite. I excluded the data of one participant from the analysis as his mean walked distance was 3SD above the mean.

I analyzed the difference scores with a univariate ANOVA with condition (control, manipulated eye height) as a between-participants factor, and difference scores as the dependent measure. The ANOVA revealed that the eye height manipulation had a significant effect on the difference scores in the manipulated group ($M = 0.09, SE = 0.01$) compared to the control group ($M = -0.003, SE = 0.02$), $F(1, 21) = 14.50, p = .001, \eta_p^2 = .41$ (see **Figure 5-6**). These results indicate that the eye height manipulation influenced the participants walked distances in the predicted direction, while there was no training effect for the control group although the individual underestimation varied between both sessions for the control group. For further analysis, I performed a paired-samples t-test for the ratio of the first and second session. I found that my participants in the manipulation group walked significantly further in the second session with the eye height manipulation ($M = 0.71, SE = 0.04$) compared to the first unaltered session ($M = 0.62, SE = 0.04$), $t(22) = -2.89, p < 0.01$ (two-tailed).

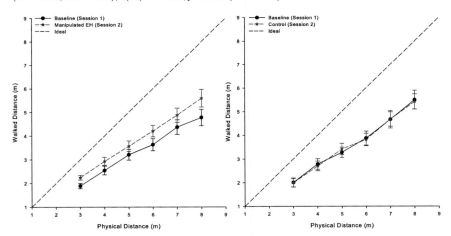

Figure 5-6: Left: The effect of a manipulated visual eye height in a sparse-cue environment in Session 2 compared to Session 1 in the test group. **Right:** There was no difference between Session 2 and Session 1 in the control group due to training. Error bars represent ±1 SE.

However, based on the prediction and corresponding calculations I expected a greater increase in perceived distances due to the lowered eye height in the second session, so that the participants would get more accurate (i.e. closer to the ideal performance). When assessing the post-experiment questionnaires, I discovered that none of the participants in the manipulated eye height group recognized the eye height change in the second session; however, they perceived the target indicating the distance to change in size. As the visual angle of the unfamiliar target object changes due to a lowered eye height, it appears larger compared to the first session, which in fact a large proportion of the participants reported. Thus, the size-distance relationship (e.g. [48], see also [188]) would indicate that the target appears closer to the observer, whereas the eye height manipulation would predict that the target is perceived as further away. Hence, the change in the visual angles subtended by the target where the participants walked to was likely counteracting the predicted effect. This could be one reason why the participants improved significantly but not as much as I expected.

5.4 Experiment 9: The Influence of the Retinal Size of the Unfamiliar Target Size

In Experiment 9, I replicated Experiment 8, with the difference that I scaled the unfamiliar target size according to the lowered eye height in the second session. If the reduced walked distances compared to ideal performance were due to changing visual angles of the target (c.f. [188]), I would expect the walked distances to be closer to the ideal performance when the target size is subtending the same visual angles throughout both sessions.

5.4.1 Method

Participants

Twelve (5 female) participants were recruited from the university community of Tübingen, Germany, and were compensated for their time at a rate of 8 € per hour. All had normal or corrected to normal visual acuity and were screened for the ability to fuse stereo displays. The age ranged from 21 to 76 years ($M = 30.31$).

Stimuli & Apparatus

For this experiment, I used the same technical setup as in Experiment 8. I used the same sparse-cue virtual environment as in Experiment 7.

Experimental Design & Procedure

All participants started the experiment by completing a written consent form, which was approved by the ethical committee of the University of Tübingen, Germany. The participants received written and verbal instructions.

I used the same design and procedure as in Experiment 8. However, for this experiment, I ensured that the visual target indicating the distances was subtending the same visual angles in the second session compared to the first session. I achieved this by scaling the target by the necessary amount based on the eye height manipulation applied in the second session.

5.4.2 Results & Discussion

I analyzed the results of Experiment 9 similar to Experiment 8 by creating ratios for the walked distances in each session by dividing the mean walked distance by the mean actual distance.

I analyzed the ratios of session one and session two using a paired-samples t-test, which revealed that the participants walked significantly further in the second session, when the eye height was manipulated ($M = 0.81, SE = 0.05$) compared to the first session without any manipulation ($M = 0.60, SE = 0.04$), $t(11) = -11.04, p < 0.001$ (two-tailed, see **Figure 5-7**). On average, the participants walked 21.8% ($SE = 0.19$) farther, which in this case equals 1.20 meters. This 1.2 meter increase was achieved by lowering the eye height of the participants by 45.4 centimeters on average. Because I used the linear approach to determine the manipulated eye height, I also predicted the walked distances in session two based on the individual underestimation for each tested distance in session one and the manipulated eye height in session two. I found that the overall calculated distances predict the observed estimates very well, $\beta = .88, t(11) = 5.83, p < .001$. The predicted distances based on the linear model and the observed underestimation in session one also explained a significant proportion of variance in the participants' distance estimates, $R^2 = .77, F(1, 11) = 40.0, p < .001$, see also the plotted predictions in **Figure 5-7**.

These results also suggest that the visual angles subtended by the target have a large impact on the perceived location of the target, as has also been suggested by results found for larger distances in the real world (e.g. [188]). These results also suggest that with a simple manipulation of the virtual eye height I can expand the perceived space in virtual environments by a considerable amount, and according to the questionnaire responses similar to Experiment 7+8, no participant recognized the eye height manipulation. Nevertheless, I also observed quite some variance in the distance estimates. While some of the participants in Experiment 2 walked 90% of the intended distance and more, others walked only 70%. However, they still improved by 20% compared to the first session, which means that even though individuals did not reach veridical performance, they considerably improved in all cases where the eye height manipulation was applied. That my participants did not perform veridically can be explained by my linear approach. The predictions explain the observed distance estimates very well when the individual underestimation from session one is taken into account. This suggests that the *extended* distance (as described in the introduction) is underestimated by a similar amount compared to the first session.

Another likely contributing factor for the underestimation of distance is that I used a sparse-cue environment, which reduced the available depth cues to a minimum and did not provide additional depth cues like familiar size. The results of Experiment 7 suggest that direct blind-walking is more accurate in a rich-cue environment compared to a reduced cue setting. This is consistent with previous work from Phillips and colleagues [144] that demonstrates a difference between blind-walking estimates in a high-fidelity virtual replica of a real room and in a wireframe-like model of the same room. However, in their setup, the wireframe-like model did not feature any ground texture, which might explain their results. In contrast, I used informative ground textures in both environments, which are likely very important for perceiving egocentric distances [137]. Thus, my visual stimuli (i.e. the rich- and sparse-cue environment) are more comparable to previous work from Kunz and colleagues [101]. Their high-fidelity IVE also provided familiar size cues, e.g. a table within the virtual room, but both of their environments

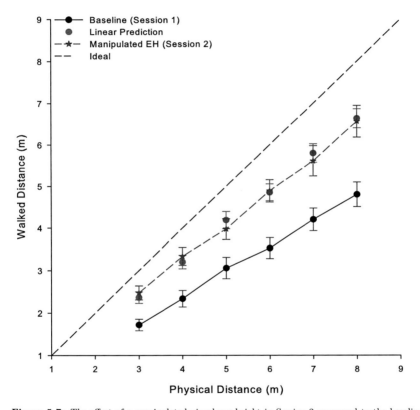

Figure 5-7: The effect of a manipulated visual eye height in Session 2 compared to the baseline (Session 1) with an adjusted distance indicating target in the sparse-cue environment. Error bars represent ±1 SE.

had informative ground textures. They found that the fidelity of the IVEs, which were similar to my environments does not influence a blind-walking measure [101]. Therefore, my findings in Experiment 7 showing that participants make more accurate blind-walking judgments when provided with a rich-cue IVE are surprising and need further investigation. This is also one of my motivations for conducting Experiment 10 in a rich-cue environment.

5.5 Experiment 10: Manipulating Eye Height to Counter Distance Underestimation in a Rich-Cue Virtual Space

To investigate whether the distance estimates with a manipulated eye height are affected by the environmental context (i.e. sparse vs. rich-cue), I replicated Experiment 9 in the rich-cue environment used in Experiment 7. This environment provides familiar size cues, lighting and shadows, which might help to assess egocentric distances in an environment and as such lead to an increased performance.

5.5.1 Method

Participants

Twelve (7 female) participants were recruited from the university community of Tübingen, Germany, and were compensated for their time at a rate of 8 € per hour. All had normal or corrected to normal visual acuity and were screened for the ability to fuse stereo displays. The age ranged from 19 to 43 years ($M = 28.17$).

Stimuli & Apparatus

For this experiment, I used the same technical setup as in Experiment 9+10. I used the rich-cue environment described in Experiment 7 to assess whether additional cues to distance have an impact on the eye height manipulation (e.g. is it more easily recognized because of the additional familiar size cues) and the accuracy of the walked distance in the second session with the manipulated eye height.

Experimental Design & Procedure

All participants started the experiment by completing a written consent form, which was approved by the ethical committee of the University of Tübingen, Germany. The participants received written and verbal instructions.

I used the same procedure and design as in Experiment 9. I also applied the same correction to the target size in the second session. However, no other cues/objects in the environment were manipulated and kept the same between both sessions.

5.5.2 Results & Discussion

For the analysis of the results for the blind-walking task in the rich-cue environment, I took a different approach compared to Experiment 9+10. In the rich-cue environment, the mean walked distance ratios were overall better in both, session one ($M = 0.88, SE = 0.06$) and session two ($M = 0.90, SE = 0.03$) compared to the sparse-cue environment used in Experiment 9, with the results of both sessions being already close to blind-walking accuracy in real world experiments.

However, there was no significant improvement from session one to session two when comparing the overall means (see **Figure 5-8**). The likely reason for this is that four participants over-walked the target distance by approximately 10% in session one. As a consequence, the algorithm raised the eye height for session two, instead of lowering it as in Experiment 8 and 9. To assess this, I investigated whether or not there was a relationship between the signed change in eye height and the change in walked distance. I found a strong correlation between the amount of the eye height difference of session two compared to session one and the individual differences in walked distance for both sessions, $r = -.887, p < .001$, which supports this prediction. This means, if the participants over-walked in session one, they walked less (and more accurately) in session two when the eye height was raised, while participants who underestimated the distance walked further (and more accurately) with a lowered eye height in the second session (see **Figure 5-9**). Furthermore, I again predicted the distances based on the individual under- or overestimation for each tested distance in session one. I found that the overall calculated distances predict the observed estimates well, $\beta = .785, t(11) = 4.0, p = .003$. The predicted distances based on the linear model and the observed underestimation in session one also explained a significant proportion of variance in the participants' distance estimates, $R^2 = .62, F(1, 11) = 16.02, p = .003$, see also the plotted predictions in **Figure 5-8**.

To quantify the improvement due to the eye height manipulations (either raising or lowering the virtual eye height), I conducted an additional analysis on the unsigned difference between the walked distances in session one and session two. A one-sample t-test indicated that the difference is reliably greater than 0 (i.e. no improvement), $t(11) = 7.53, p < 0.001$ (two-tailed). This means, the distance estimates of the participants improved significantly towards veridical performance with the eye height manipulation applied. On average the participants improved by 10% ($SE = 0.01$) towards veridical performance due to an average change in eye height of 25 cm, regardless of the overall good performance across the participants. Surprisingly, the questionnaire responses revealed that no participant recognized the applied eye height manipulation in the second session, although many familiar size cues were present in the IVE.

When comparing the overall mean in the second session, the participants achieved already a performance of 90% with the same linear eye height manipulation as in Experiment 2, which is close to different real world results over the tested distance range (e.g. 95% in [113]). However, the two environments differed not only in the rendering quality (e.g. shadows and light mapping versus none) but also differed drastically in content. While the sparse-cue environment did not provide any cues to distance except the angle of declination, a textured ground surface, the horizon and linear perspective in an open area, the rich-cue environment included a wealth of cues informative about distances in a small, enclosed virtual office space. Thus, it is likely that the presence of additional cues in the rich-cue compared to the sparse-cue environments has an impact on the walked distances. Furthermore, the underestimation in the rich-cue environment was considerably less compared to the one observed in the sparse-cue environment, thus in turn,

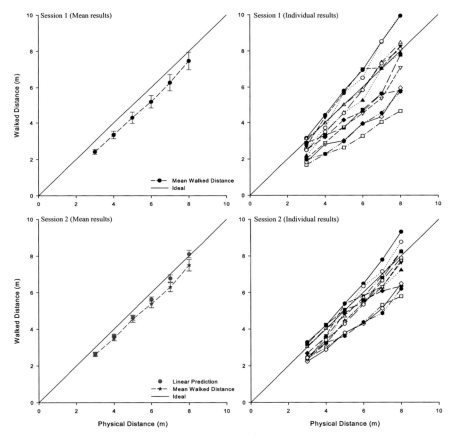

Figure 5-8: Left: Mean walked distances across all participants for session one *(top)* and session two *(bottom)* in the rich-cue environment with the solid lines in both graphs indicate veridical performance. Error bars represent ±1 SE. **Right:** The individual results of all twelve participants plotted with the solid line indicating ideal performance. All participants improved considerably towards veridical performance in session two *(bottom)* compared to session one *(top)* due to the applied eye height manipulation.

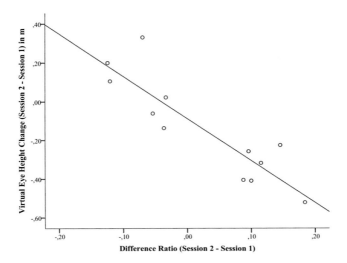

Figure 5-9: Correlation illustrating the link between the amount of the eye height difference in session two compared to session one and the individual differences in walked distance in both sessions. Participants with a lowered eye height in session two walked further while participants with a raised eye height in session two walked shorter.

the amount of eye height manipulation required to reduce or eliminate this underestimation is less. Nevertheless, further investigation will be required to find the main reason for my results concerning the performance in the two different VEs.

In the rich-cue environment I observed over-walking, which is a rare occurrence in virtual reality distance perception studies. In real world studies, over-walking is quite common (e.g. [116]), where the participants achieve a veridical performance on average, but some tend to slightly over-walk the distances. While, this over-estimation is a rare occurrence in IVEs, the results suggest that the eye height manipulation is not only an effective tool to reduce distance underestimation in virtual environments, but can also be very effective to compensate for overestimation, which makes it well suited for user-centric applications. In fact, eight out of the twelve participants achieved an accuracy of 88% or better, with four participants achieving a veridical performance (i.e. 100% of the intended distance) in the second session with the eye height manipulation applied (see **Figure 5-8**). Thus, in an ecologically valid virtual environment with sufficient visual cues, the eye height manipulation based on the linear prediction seems already to allow users to judge distances very close as they would in the real world, although I did not consider that the underestimation likely also applies to the *extended distance* in the second session.

5.6 Experiment 11: Manipulating Eye Height Factoring in Underestimation

Experiments 9 and 10 provided evidence that distance underestimation can be drastically reduced, even very close to performance which is usually observed in the real world (c.f. Experiment 10), and that this performance can be predicted quite accurately. The fit of the predictions based on the linear prediction (as investigated in Experiments 2 and 3) suggests that eye height manipulations are a valuable tool to selectively reduce distance underestimation in IVEs. Thus, individual veridical performance should be possible when the underestimation is already considered for determining the necessary virtual eye height manipulation. To investigate whether this can be achieved, I conducted another experiment where the manipulated eye height is calculated by also considering the observed underestimation in session one (multiplicative prediction). As described in the introduction, to fully eliminate 20% distance underestimation, the virtual eye height manipulation needs to be calculated by considering that a similar underestimation applies to the *extended distance*. Thus, a 25% extended distance is theoretically necessary to eliminate 20% underestimation as the extended distance will itself be underestimated by 20%. This in practice means that the virtual eye eye height needs to be lowered by 20% to compensate for 20% underestimation.

5.6.1 Method

Participants

Twenty (10 female) participants were recruited from the university community of Tübingen, Germany, and were compensated for their time at a rate of 8 € per hour. All had normal or corrected to normal visual acuity and were screened for the ability to fuse stereo displays. The age ranged from 20 to 38 years ($M = 26.2$).

Stimuli & Apparatus

For this experiment, I used the same technical setup as in Experiment 10. For this experiment I used both environments (each participant was only assigned to one), the sparse- and rich-cue environment. For both groups I used the multiplicative prediction as described in the introduction of this chapter, where the eye height is lowered more to compensate for the fact that the new distance will likely also be underestimated.

Experimental Design & Procedure

All participants started the experiment by completing a written consent form, which was approved by the ethical committee of the University of Tübingen, Germany. The participants received written and verbal instructions.

I used the same design and procedure as in Experiments 9 and 10. Each participant was randomly assigned to only one environment (between-participant design).

5.6.2 Results & Discussion

I analyzed the results of Experiment 11 similar to Experiment 10 by creating ratios for the walked distances in each session by dividing the mean walked distance by the mean actual distance. For simplicity, the analysis is described separately for each environment.

Sparse-cue environment: I analyzed the ratios of session one and session two using a paired-samples t-test, which revealed that the participants walked significantly farther in the second session when the eye height was manipulated ($M = 0.88, SE = 0.02$) compared to the first session without any manipulation ($M = 0.70, SE = 0.04$), $t(9) = -4.02, p = 0.004$ (two-tailed, see **Figure 5-10**). On average, the participants in the sparse-cue environment walked 17.77% further, which equals 0.98 meters more distance walked in the mean (actual mean of all tested distances was 5.5 meters). However, by using the multiplicative prediction I expected that the distance estimates would be on average veridical (e.g. very close to 100%, see predictions in **Figure 5-10**), because it considers the observed individual mean underestimation in session one for the calculation of the eye height manipulation.

Rich-cue environment: Similar to the sparse-cue environment I analyzed the ratios of session one and session two using a paired-samples t-test, which revealed that the participants walked significantly further in the second session also in the rich-cue environment, where the eye height was manipulated ($M = 0.89, SE = 0.05$) compared to the first session without any manipulation ($M = 0.82, SE = 0.05$), $t(9) = -2.82, p = 0.04$ (two-tailed, see **Figure 5-11**). On average, the participants in the sparse-cue environment walked 7% further, which equals 0.39 meters more distance walked in the mean (actual mean of all tested distances was 5.5 meters). Similar to the sparse-cue environment, I expected that the distance estimates would be veridical on average (see predictions in **Figure 5-11**) when using the multiplicative approach.

In both environments, the distance estimates were close to the performance observed in the real world using the same action-based measure, however, when considering the predictions, the participants in both environments did not walk as far as intended. There might be multiple reasons why I observed this effect. First of all, I observed that the manipulation, although calculated for each participant individually, had different effects on the participants in both environments. For example, some participants improved by very large amounts and achieved veridical performance on average (see the examples in **Figure 5-12**). Others improved also by very large amounts (e.g. one participant walked 47% in session one and 82% with the eye height manipulation applied, an increase of 35%), but did not reach close to veridical performance and some participants only improved marginally (e.g. from 67% of the walked distance to 73%). Thus, it is possible that the eye height manipulation might influence some individuals differently, although the performance of all participants improved.

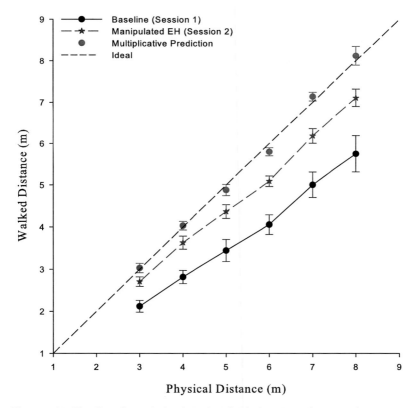

Figure 5-10: The effect of a manipulated visual eye height factoring in distance underestimation in Session 2 compared to the baseline (Session 1) in the sparse-cue environment. Error bars represent ±1 SE.

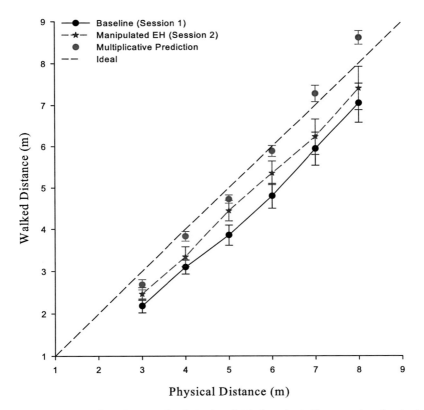

Figure 5-11: The effect of a manipulated visual eye height factoring in distance underestimation in Session 2 compared to the baseline (Session 1) in the sparse-cue environment. Error bars represent ±1 SE.

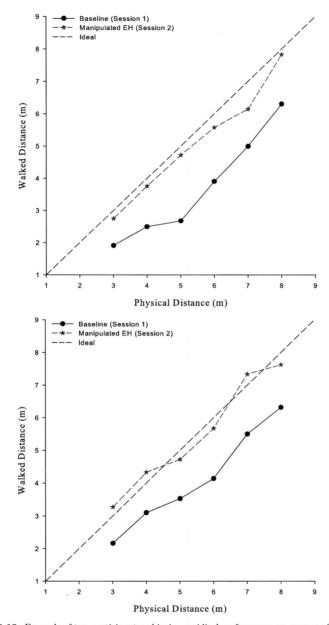

Figure 5-12: Example of two participants achieving veridical performance on average after the eye height manipulation (multiplicative) is applied.

In fact, when analyzing the questionnaires, I recognized that Experiment 11 was the first experiment, where a larger portion of the participants noticed the eye height manipulation, which in this study was rather large due to the multiplicative approach. For example, consider that a participant with an eye height of 1.65 meters underestimates the distance by 50%. Based on the linear prediction and assuming a target at a distance of 5 meters, the new manipulated virtual eye height would be 1.10 meters (i.e. a lowering by 55 centimeters, similar to the eye height variations in Experiment 1). Now consider the same example if one wants to account for the fact that the 2.5 meters will also be 50% underestimated. This means, based on the multiplicative prediction, the corresponding manipulated eye height would be 0.825 meters, which requires to lower the virtual eye height by 82.5 centimeters (that is 50% of the actual eye height). Given the questionnaire results, it is likely that there are some limitations of how far eye height can be altered to reduce distance underestimation in IVEs.

Furthermore, while all experiments support the notion that manipulating eye height is a valuable tool to reduce or in many cases to even eliminate distance underestimation, the experiments presented here have also some limitations, which could have contributed to my obtained results. Specifically, I considered only the overall mean underestimation to determine the eye height manipulation (linear and multiplicative), however, underestimation can vary strongly even within the different tested distances and trials. Thus, the effect of the manipulated eye height may vary between the single target distances. Furthermore, for the calculation of the manipulated eye height, the actual eye height of the participant is necessary. To assess the actual eye height in the HMD, I used the mean eye height during the exploration phase in the first session. It was calculated based on the tracking data of the used optical tracking system, because the participant was not allowed to walk or bend and it very closely matched the measured standing eye height of the participant. However, it might have been better to have access to the exact eye height value when the participant decided on the distance. As eye height can easily vary a couple of centimeters by just scanning the ground plane, this adds some undesired variability, which might contribute to the variance regarding the improvement due to the manipulated eye height between the participants.

5.7 Summary & Discussion

With this set of studies, I have shown that eye height is a powerful metric for the scaling of distances, that can be exploited to create desired percepts in IVEs. In Experiment 7, I replicated the results of the previous experiments, which showed that eye height seems to be determined by body-based cues when sensory information specifying eye height is in conflict. In addition, the results of this experiment revealed that eye height manipulations influence both, an action-based response measure, direct blind-walking, in the same manner as verbal reports .

Most importantly, I have also shown that because humans rely on their body-based eye height, this can be exploited to expand (or compress) the perceived space, without the necessity of expensive equipment, feedback or training, and minification as in other approaches (c.f. [133, 230, 98, 97, 162]). Specifically, I have shown that a simple eye height manipulation can be used to expand perceived distances on an individual basis (Experiment 8-11). Thereby, I have also shown, that the retinal size of an unfamiliar distance indicating object/target can have a large impact on perceived egocentric distances (Experiment 8-9), which might be an indicator for the strong influence that the retinal size of unfamiliar objects can have on the perception of the spatial layout of our environment (see [188] for a real world example). When combining the results of Experiment 9-11, I found, that eye height manipulations are not only an effective tool to reduce or even counter distance underestimation, but also for countering the rarely occurring overestimation of perceived distance in IVEs. In addition, the results of Experiments 10+11 are very similar to results achieved in real world experiments (e.g. [34, 115]). This means that a virtual environment combined with an eye height manipulation to drastically reduce individual distance underestimation seems to be a very promising approach to enable individuals to accurately perceive the spatial layout of an IVE.

Interestingly, I also found that the walked distances differed depending on the environment (c.f. Experiment 7). As previous work has suggested that the quality of graphics only affects verbal reports [101] but not direct blind-walking [202, 101], the reason for the increased performance in the rich-cue environment might be that the additional cues to distance in the used environment like light, shadows and familiar size cues along with the angle of declination below the horizon are helpful to decrease the usually observed distance underestimation.

With this work, I have shown that a simple eye height manipulation can alter the perceived space in IVEs and as such be used to achieve a close to veridical perception of distances, which is useful for many applications. In contrast to other attempts to counter distance underestimation in IVEs (e.g. [230, 98]), the applied eye height manipulation maintains more of the perceptual fidelity of visual aspects of the IVE, because it works with less drastic effects on many visual cues present in a virtual environment. However, an open question remains: Eye height is known to be very important for perceiving the height of objects in the visual field [224, 225]. Thus, further research needs to investigate, how the perceived height of different objects is affected by an eye height manipulation in IVEs, which is not only true for this approach but also for other approaches like minification [98, 230], where every visual angle of an object is altered, theoretically changing its perceived size.

Nevertheless, my work has several implications for egocentric distance judgments in HMD-based IVEs. First of all, the presented work emphasizes the importance of a correct calibration of the HMD regarding eye height. Any miscalibration regarding the virtual eye height will likely have effects on the perceived spatial layout of the environment. Specifically, for setups where no accurate head tracking can be provided, it is important to measure the physical eye height of the observer and to adjust the virtual camera accordingly to provide comparable conditions for all participants of a different height. However if this is not possible, with the theoretical framework provided in this and my previous experiments, it is possible to quantify the effect, which a discrepancy between virtual and real eye height has on perceived distances.

My work has also practical implications by contributing to previous work trying to counter distance underestimation in IVEs, which is important for several applications that rely on spatial perception mirroring that in the real world. In comparison to previous work using, for example, minification, I show that manipulating the virtual eye height can be a solution with comparable effects on perceived distances, but with consistent effects across different measures. In addition, my approach employing a manipulated eye height is easy to implement and can be applied on an individual basis to control for the apriori misperception present (e.g. over- or underestimation). Thus, this approach might be usable in practical scenarios, for example in design reviews. The eye height manipulation can be based on an individual's previous performance (or might be determined in a very short time frame, e.g. with some simple judgments) to enable every user an experience close to what was intended by the programmer of the VE.

Chapter 6

General Discussion

In this chapter I will summarize the findings of the various experiments described in this dissertation and how they relate to the research questions presented in chapter 3. Furthermore, I will discuss the findings in the context of related literature from both, perceptual psychology and computer science perspectives. Finally, I will discuss further questions concerning the presented work in this thesis and highlight possibilities for future work.

6.1 Summary of the Empirical Results

The first set of experiments presented in chapter 4 in this thesis supports the hypothesis that eye height is informed by body-based cues. In the experiments where I manipulated the visual eye height to decouple the visual and body-based eye height of the observer, I found an influence on perceived distance as would be predicted if the participants relied more on their body-based cues. Specifically, in Experiment 1, the group of participants who experienced the lowered visual eye height, with respect to their own eye height when standing, overestimated distances compared to the participants, who experienced the virtual world from their actual eye height. Furthermore, when the eye height was raised, distances were underestimated compared to the baseline and appeared very close to what would be predicted by the angle of declination if eye height would be informed by body-based cues. This hypothesis was supported in Experiment 2, where I observed similar results in a sitting posture, which also indicates that eye height is informed by changes in posture. Nevertheless, one could argue that standing and sitting are the most experienced postures, and eye height could also be informed by experience. However, Experiment 3 showed that experience, at least in VR, is likely not responsible for informing eye height by showing that eye height is informed by body-based cues even in irregular postures. Another question that was important to consider was whether people can reliably estimate their own visual eye height in the real and virtual world.

In Experiment 4, I tested whether the visual information present in IVEs would actually be sufficient to inform eye height appropriately or whether the participants relied on body-based cues to inform their eye height due to unreliable visual information. The results of the adjustment task indicate that on average the participants could accurately judge their eye height based on the available visual information in the different IVEs. Thus, these results refute the notion that participants only relied on their body-based cues when visual information is insufficient. Nevertheless, individual variability was quite high, which could indicate why the perceptual system incorporates body-based information into the determination of eye height. This variability is not likely due to the limitations of HMD-based IVEs (e.g. an accommodation-convergence mismatch), as I show in two real world experiments.

The results of Experiment 5 provide further evidence that internalized knowledge is not used to inform eye height as it is unlikely that participants have a wealth of previous experience standing on a ramp of that height. In addition, the eye height judgment task in Experiment 5 yielded similar results in the real world compared to Experiment 4 in IVEs, namely accurate judgments on average with a quite high individual variability. Finally, the results of Experiment 6 provide further evidence that body-based cues can also be used in the real world to inform eye height and that these effects are not only due to a potentially diminished reliability of visual information in IVEs. Specifically, the results align very closely with my predictions based on body-based eye height, while the obtained eye height judgments again show a similar pattern as previously found in IVEs: accurate judgments on average with large individual variability. Hence, this poorly specified visual eye height cannot account for the influences on the distance estimates. Indeed, if visually specified eye height is highly variable in normal daily situations, it would make sense to rely on other senses to determine eye height instead.

Thus, with this first set of experiments presented in Chapter 3 in this thesis, I show that there are cases where eye height is informed by body-based cues more than by visual information as would be predicted by popular theories in visual perception (Hypothesis 1). Furthermore, I also show that eye height is informed by changes in posture, as long they are aligned with the gravity vector (i.e. Experiments 1-3,5), to ensure an unchanging perception of our surrounding environment across different postures in the real and more importantly in virtual worlds (Hypothesis 2). Furthermore, the observed reliance on body-based cues for informing eye height is not limited to virtual worlds, but can also be observed in a real world environment, which contains a wealth of visual information (Hypothesis 3). Thus, the use of body-based cues to inform eye height is likely consistent across environments (as it also occurs in the real world). This means, that despite future improvements of VR technology, the users will likely rely on their body-based cues to inform eye height, which makes the research presented in this dissertation valuable regardless of technology advancements.

While these results are already very surprising with respect to perceptual theories, they also form the foundation for the engineering motivation in this dissertation, as all of the previously mentioned hypotheses have practical implications for the use of IVEs. From the engineering perspective, it is important to understand the perceptual consequences in IVEs if virtual eye height deviates from the actual eye height of an observer, as well as whether virtual eye height manipulations can be a valuable tool to manipulate space perception in IVEs.

In Experiment 7 I investigated whether the found effects on perceived distances also generalize to other measures like a commonly used action-based measure, i.e. direct blind-walking. The results are very similar to those obtained using verbal reports (Experiments 1-3), suggesting that the changes in the distance judgments are due to a changed perception of the space rather than a cognitive decision to change responses. In sum, the reliance on body-based cues to inform eye height has similar consequences across different measures, and as a result, eye height manipulations should be capable of countering individuals' distance underestimation in IVEs. The results of Experiment 8 suggest that while the individual eye height manipulation had the predicted effect of reducing distance underestimation, the size of the effect was much smaller than expected. Because the participants reported that the target seems to change the size, I adjusted the target to maintain the same retinal size across the sessions in Experiment 9. With this change the manipulation of virtual eye height based on the individual underestimation had a large effect resulting in close to veridical distance judgments. The judgments with the compensatory eye height manipulation applied corresponded very closely to the predictions when taking into account the individual underestimation for calculating the predictions. Experiment 10, conducted in a different VE confirmed that eye height is a valuable tool to not only reduce or counter distance underestimation but also to correct for overestimation. All participants walked closer to the intended distances after an eye height manipulation was applied, reaching close to veridical performance on average. In addition, the values calculated based on the individual underestimation and the applied eye height manipulation accurately predict the performance of each participant (as close as to three centimeters!). Finally, in Experiment 11 I tested the eye height manipulation while additionally taking into account that underestimation also affects the new indicated distances due to an eye height manipulation. The results correspond very closely to the previous experiments with participants achieving a very similar performance as observed in the real world. Nevertheless, based on the larger eye height manipulation I would have predicted veridical performance, which I did not observe. The reason might be that these eye height manipulations were too large: there might be some limitations for the amount the virtual eye height can be manipulated, while achieving the predicted effects on perceived distances.

In summary, the results of this second set of experiments show that because eye height is mainly informed by body-based cues, virtual eye height manipulations are an easy, useful, and valuable tool to reduce the observed distance underestimation in IVEs (Hypothesis 4) and to manipulate space perception (see e.g. [39][35]). Surprisingly, this manipulation is usually not noticed by the observer (depending on the amount, manipulations larger than approx. 75 centimeters were often noticed, see Experiment 11), which might make eye height manipulations a useful tool in many applied scenarios. Furthermore, the effect of a manipulated eye height on perceived distance is consistent across different measures, which might make eye height manipulations a valuable tool for reducing distance underestimation regardless of how the IVE is assessed. Moreover, the results also suggest that in VR setups, where the virtual eye height cannot be adjusted easily to the actual eye height of the observer, the effects of such a mismatch can be quite accurately predicted by the underlying theory presented in this dissertation. Thereby, I also show, that the virtual eye height has major implications for many existing VR setups.

---

[35]See also www.vr-hyperspace.eu for a research project where the results of this dissertation are employed to manipulate perceived space.

6.2 The Importance of Body-Based Information in Visual Perception

One main goal of the research conducted in this dissertation was to investigate what sensory information is used to inform eye height. I used VR technology to decouple the naturally coincident sources of information potentially specifying eye height and found that if those sources are in conflict, body-based cues dominate over visual cues to inform eye height. This finding was also replicated in a real world setting: this excludes the possibility that body-based cues are only used in an experimental setting where visual information might not be as reliable in the real world.

Thus, this research extends previous research which has speculated about how eye height is informed. Specifically, other researchers suggested (in different contexts) that eye height is body-scaled information that is informed by *intrinsic* information (e.g. [123, 208]), although they were vague about what this intrinsic information actually might be. With this work I provide the first empirical evidence that this intrinsic information likely consists of body-based cues and that this sensory information is also used to inform eye height across different postures. The finding that eye height is appropriately informed by changes in posture to ensure an unchanging environment, e.g. when sitting and then standing up. These findings complement previous research from Wraga, where she found that the perception of object sizes is constant throughout a change in posture [225]. The results of these experiments suggest that not only are the perceptions of object sizes remain constant following a change in posture, but also the perceived distance to an object (a target on the floor in this case).

These results are also important in the context of recently conducted research (as discussed in Chapter 4). Considering Bingham and colleagues [139, 31] recently published research which they interpret to support the notion that eye height is informed by stereo information that needs to be calibrated (by performing actions over time) for accurate reaching performance when eye height is changing, the experimental results in this thesis are surprising. I found that eye height can be informed by body-based cues without any calibration. However, it is important to consider their definition of eye height. They define eye height as the distance from the eyes to a support surface (i.e. a table), and when the height of this support surface varies, this new height between the eyes and the table needs to calibrated over time. While it seems that the results presented in this dissertation appear to contradict these recent results, this is not necessarily true. In fact, the seated eye height of the observer (i.e. the eyes to the ground) never changes in their experimental paradigm and this seated eye height (i.e. eyes to the ground) defines the eye height unit. Thus, the height of the table is likely represented as a specific proportion of the eye height unit, and as this proportion can constantly change, for example by manipulating the table height, the observer needs to calibrate to this new proportion: this is where depth cues to the table surface likely play an important role [31, 139]. Nevertheless, the eye height unit defined by the seated observer can still be informed by body-based cues as argued in this thesis. Conducting a series of studies combining both experimental paradigms (the one used for the reaching studies and the one used throughout this dissertation) would be interesting to investigate whether both predictions hold true.

Finally, the results of the experiments investigating what sensory information is used to determine eye height challenge traditional theories in visual perception, which infer that visual information is dominant and that the visual perceptual system does not incorporate any other information from other modalities to create our visual perceptions of the surrounding environment [158]. The findings presented in this thesis demonstrate a case where a fundamental visual task like distance perception is accomplished by combining information from different sensory modalities, which refutes the common assumptions in traditional perceptual theories that visual information is dominant [149]. However, these are not the first results challenging this view. The empirical work in this thesis complements other studies, demonstrating, for example, that body-based cues can dominate when estimating walked distances [22], or that body-based cues are important for navigation in an environment (e.g. [206]). Other research has even demonstrated that emotional variables like fear can influence our visual perception of heights (see for example [190, 191, 30]), arguing for alternative approaches such as a multi-sensory integration approach [49], where different sensory cues are weighted and integrated according to their reliability for a given task. The experimental results presented in this thesis can likely also be explained by such an approach, however with the chosen experimental design, it is not possible to fully disentangle what I refer to as body-based cues in addition to other potentially contributing information like vision.

In summary, the studies presented in this dissertation complement other research, demonstrating the importance of body-based cues in the context of visual perception. In addition, these results support the notion that also other sensory information than visual information are important to our perception of the spatial layout of our surrounding environment.

6.3 Understanding Visual Perception to Increase the Utility of VR

The applied goal of the research presented in this dissertation was to investigate the effect of virtual eye height on perceived distances and whether virtual eye height manipulations are a valuable tool to reduce or even counter distance underestimation in IVEs. With the previously discussed findings, that eye height is mainly informed by body-based cues if the sensory information specifying eye height is in conflict, I was able to demonstrate that eye height manipulations alter the perceived distances in an IVE in a predictable way. However, not only the influence on perceived distances (i.e. under or overestimation) can be predicted; based on the assumption that eye height is informed almost exclusively by body-based cues, it is possible to quite accurately predict how perceived distances within an IVE will change due to a virtual eye height which deviates from the actual eye height of the user. Thus, the presented research can also be used to predict biases in perceived distances throughout VR systems, where an accurate eye height calibration is not possible. However, the presented research is not the first work to investigate specific aspects of perception in IVEs to improve the utility of VR.

This research complements and extends other work which tries to counter the commonly observed distance underestimation within VEs, like for example providing feedback [129, 130, 161, 162], minification [97, 98, 230], using transitional environments [192] or providing a self-avatar [132, 133, 164, 145]. But how does the approach to improve distance perception in this thesis compare to other approaches? Considering a feedback approach, there is compelling evidence that providing feedback or specifically the possibility for calibration can improve distance judgments in IVEs. However, this usually requires some interaction with the IVE, which is not always possible in many VR systems and is very time consuming. Furthermore, this interaction within an IVE can have adverse effects on the perception in the real world (see for example [162]), which might limit the usability of such approaches in diverse applied scenarios. While the minification approach seems very promising [97, 98, 230], because it is easy to use and implement, it is not clear yet whether this manipulation can be applied to reduce distance underestimation on an individual basis or whether the compensatory distortion to the entire environment has adverse consequences to other percepts. Theoretically, it should be possible to previously measure the individual underestimation and then minify the virtual image accordingly. Nevertheless, it is not clear yet, whether and how the relationship between perceived distances and minification can be modeled to be able to predict the necessary amount of minification based on specific underestimation. Furthermore, it seems that cognitive and action based measures are affected differently (see [230]), which is surprising because all visual depth cues are altered in the virtual world. This should have similar effects on different measures. Similarly, due to the visually distorted environment, it is an open question how this warping of depth cues influences other variables, especially considering that a correct rendering of the view is judged as more natural by naive participants [193], while the eye height manipulation was not recognized in almost all of my experiments.

Other solutions to reduce distance underestimation in IVEs employ transitional environments to improve distance perception within IVEs. However, in contrast to the approach proposed in this dissertation, it is not really clear yet what causes the improvement of the distance judgments and how this can specifically be tailored to enable every user to perceive the IVE like intended by the content designer. Further research is necessary to investigate whether transitional environments can be a tool to reduce the commonly observed distance underestimation in IVEs.

Finally, one approach which has triggered a lot of interest is to provide the user with a self-animated avatar in the IVE. Preliminary evidence indicates that avatars can improve perceived distance in virtual environments [132, 133, 164, 145], although the necessary and sufficient conditions for this are not fully understood and the results are inconclusive. Although Mohler and colleagues [133] provide compelling evidence that providing an avatar is sufficient to achieve veridical performance in an IVE, further research is necessary to investigate how the user must be represented in the virtual world that this representation has the desired effect on perceived distances. Moreover, providing the user with a fully-animated self-representing avatar is currently not a trivial task. It requires expensive motion capture equipment, highly refined software, sophisticated 3-D models of the human body with a rigged skeleton, all of which require a great deal of money, time and specialized expertise. Nevertheless, my previous work has shown that an eye height manipulation can also be applied when the user is represented by an avatar (see [109]), with comparable effects to the results obtained throughout the experiments presented in this thesis. Thus, a combination of these approaches might be a promising venue for further research.

In summary, the approach presented in this dissertation has some advantages over other approaches to reduce or counter distance underestimation in IVEs. Furthermore, the eye height manipulation approach should be usable across different VR systems and not only in HMD-based IVEs. Preliminary evidence suggests that this can also be used in LSIDs, as pointed out by Franz in his dissertation. He found an influence of the viewpoint on perceived distances when he investigated the utility of VR for architectural simulations [60]. Nevertheless, the approach presented in this dissertation does have some limitations. While some limitations are common to all approaches, like the variability in human distance perception and the corresponding variability in distance underestimation, other limitations/further questions apply specifically for the approach presented in this dissertation. These questions and potential future work are discussed in the next section.

6.4 Further Questions and Future Work

With the research presented in this dissertation, I have found that eye height for perceiving egocentric distances can be informed by body-based cues and that eye height is also informed appropriately by changes in the posture. This reliance on body-based cues extends also to real world scenarios and can be exploited to reduce the commonly observed distance underestimation in IVEs by manipulating the virtual eye height according to the relationship of eye height and the angle of declination below the horizon. However, there are still further questions related to the presented research, which could inspire future work to explore these questions. Some of these questions and potential corresponding future work will be outlined in the following:

What is the influence of feedback/calibration? All presented experiments in this thesis were conducted without giving the participants feedback about their distance estimates or the possibility to calibrate themselves to the altered visual information, because this is a likely scenario in many applied settings, where the possibilities for interaction are limited due to the VR setup. Nevertheless, recent research argues that eye height with respect to a support surface (e.g. a table) requires calibration over time by executing different actions (e.g. a reach) on the support surface [31, 139, 13]. Also other researchers have argued and demonstrated that calibration may be necessary for accurate actions in a given environment [166, 12]. The participants in my experiments reached close to veridical performance when measured with an action-based measure and an eye height manipulation applied, even without any feedback or possibility to calibrate themselves to the altered visual information. However, it is an open question how this potential additional information about eye height from feedback would affect perceived distances when the sensory information specifying eye height is decoupled (i.e. a different visual eye height than indicated from body-based cues). Thus, for potential future work it would be interesting to see whether a feedback paradigm (like in for example [161, 162, 129, 166, 31, 139]) would change how eye height is determined, i.e. whether the visual information is becoming more reliable. This could be achieved by giving participants the possibility to really walk around with a manipulated eye height before testing their distance perception in the explored VE. If they calibrate to the altered visual information, due to the received visuo-motor feedback by walking around, visual information might become more abundant as well as reliable and the observers might rely more on this information. Further work is necessary to investigate whether this is actually true or whether humans still rely more on their body-based senses to inform eye height.

How is perceived size influenced by a virtual eye height manipulation? It is well known that eye height, or more specifically the eye height ratio, is fundamental to perceive the sizes of object in our environment, also across different postures (e.g. see [224, 225]). It is unclear how a manipulated virtual eye height affects the perceived size of objects within the VE when eye height is determined by body-based cues. In principle, the altered virtual eye height might have similar effects as for example the false floor in Wraga's study (objects were judged as larger when the hidden floor was moved up), demonstrating that the eye height ratio is used to determine the sizes of different object [225]. Then I would expect that when lowering the virtual eye height that objects are estimated as larger and when the eye height is raised objects will appear smaller (similar to what was observed by Dixon and colleagues [41][36]). Thus, it is possible that there might be undesired side effects on perceived size in IVEs. Further studies are necessary to investigate how perceived size is influenced by a manipulation of the virtual eye height, especially in the context of the eye height manipulation applied for the experiments in this dissertation. In fact, almost none of the participants noticed the altered eye height, thus how this altered eye height changes size remains an open question. However, similar concerns apply also to other approaches to reduce distance underestimation in IVEs like for example minification [97, 98, 230], where every single visual angle of each object in the scene is altered, theoretically changing its perceived size.

Are other variables affected by the manipulation? Similar to the question whether a manipulation of the virtual eye height influences the perceived size of different objects, this manipulation could also have an influence on other variables, like the overall scale of the virtual space or for example affordances. Indeed, in previous work, I found that the eye height manipulation also changes the perceived dimensions (i.e. length, width and height) of a virtual replica of an office, see [109]. However, this might even be a desirable side effect. Considering my previous work, the mentioned room dimensions were all underestimated

---

[36]Although they conducted their experiments in immersive and non-immersive displays, their manipulation of eye height it not really clear. From the statement in their article, it is not clear whether they adjusted the virtual horizon or really the virtual eye height: "To specify the placement of the virtual horizon, each observer's eye height was measured in centimeters with a metric measuring tape and entered into the computer program that generated the virtual world" [41]. Thus their observed influence might not stem from a manipulation to the virtual eye height, but more from a manipulation to the virtual horizon, which according to the horizon-ratio also changes perceived size (as also shown for perceived distances, see [128, 159]).

in the baseline condition where the virtual eye height matched the actual eye height of the participant. This means that not only the judged egocentric distances were underestimated as expected, but also the room dimension as judged by length, width and height of the room were underestimated. With an altered virtual eye height all three estimates were close to veridical, indicating a shift in the overall scale of the environment. Thus, the applied eye height manipulation enabled the participants to perceive the virtual world like intended by the programmer. However, further studies are necessary to investigate whether this finding can be replicated across different environments. If this is the case, the virtual eye height manipulation would not only be an easy to use and implement tool to reduce distance underestimation but may actually have the benefit that other aspects of the spatial layout of the surrounding environment are also affected by this manipulation in a desired way. Furthermore, eye height manipulations might even be usable to further manipulate perceived space in IVEs (see [39])

Are there boundaries for a manipulation of the virtual eye height? The individual underestimation of distances in IVEs can drastically vary between different individuals. When for example measured with an action-based measure some people walk 90% of the intended distance, while others underestimate drastically and walk only 50% of the intended distance. Thus, the eye height manipulation required for the first example is somewhat small (i.e. 17 cm for an observer with 1.70 m eye height and assuming the multiplicative approach, see Chapter 5), the one for the second example rather large (i.e. 85 cm with the aforementioned assumptions). Although in all experiments, except Experiment 11, no participant overtly noticed the eye height manipulation in the VE. Hence, there might be a natural boundary by how much the virtual eye height can be altered to still achieve the desired effects. For example, previous research has investigated the utility of eye height scaling for estimating the sizes of different objects [226]. Wraga & Proffitt found that there is an upper and lower limit for the usability of eye height to scale size (e.g. from 0.2 times the observers standing eye height to 2.5 times the standing eye height, see [226]). Thus, it is possible, that similar ranges apply for the usability of a manipulation to the virtual eye height. Future work could investigate if there are such boundaries for the virtual eye height and where these boundaries are. Furthermore, there are of course limitations implied by applications potentially using such manipulations. In his dissertation, Franz investigated architectural simulations using VR technology and suggested that eye height manipulations might be a valuable tool to improve the perception of virtual spaces in such a context [60]. However, in such an applied context there are some boundaries for a potential manipulation of eye height and Franz notes that "the useful variation range spans approximately from the height of furniture surfaces which are normally seen from above (approx. 1.20 m) to the pass line height of doors (approx. 2 m). Within these limits, virtual eye height offers a considerable potential to adjust the perception of dimensions and distances", see [60]. Nevertheless, this proposed range is already sufficient to alter the perceived space by large amounts as demonstrated in this thesis.

Chapter 7

Implications of the Current Work

The research presented in this dissertation has several implications from both, a theoretical and an applied perspective. In the following sections I will discuss these implications and how the work presented in this thesis contributes to both, the field of computer science and perceptual psychology.

7.1 Novel Theoretical Implications

While the main goal of this dissertation was to investigate the influence of eye height to improve the utility of IVEs, particularly the perception of distances within IVEs, the research in this dissertation has also several implications from a theoretical viewpoint regarding visual perception. In fact, the results presented in this dissertation are surprising, because they indicate that our body contributes important information to what was usually considered a purely visual task. Furthermore, these findings suggest that this body-based information is combined with visual information (the angle of declination) to form a coherent percept of our surrounding environment. According to a dominant theory in visual perception, this combination is unlikely. For example Pylyshyn argues that the process of transforming optical information into a percept is isolated from influences of other, non-optical information [158]. However, the research in this thesis challenges this view by demonstrating that the eye height variable is informed by body-based cues and not solely visual information, and that this eye height is combined with visual information to perceive egocentric distances. Thus, the research in this thesis implies that other senses (here the body-based senses) can contribute important information for perceiving our environment, even though no perceptual-locomotor feedback or possibility for calibration was provided.

In general, the notion that using body-based cues for perceiving spatial properties of our environment is not new, however, such influences usually were found in walking paradigms [23, 22], where proprioceptive information can be dominant when estimating the walked distance. However, I found that body-based information can also be dominant over visual information even if no walking is involved. Furthermore, the results and predictions in chapter 5 indicate that body-based cues are not only dominant, but used almost exclusively to determine eye height. The predictions have a very good fit to the obtained data (especially Expriment 9 and 10), and those predictions are based on the assumption that the observers relied to a very large degree on the body-based senses to determine eye height instead of vision.

However, in the context of multi-sensory integration this may not be too surprising. When investigating, for example how the information from looking at an object, while simultaneously exploring the object with the hand is integrated, Ernst & Banks found that "humans integrate visual and haptic information in a statistically optimal fashion" [49]. That means, that the nervous system combines both sources of information (visual and haptic) about the object in a maximum-likelihood way. In their case, visual information was dominant over the touch information only when the variance in the visual estimation is lower than that of the haptic estimation [49]. In the context of the highly variable visual estimates of eye height in this thesis, it would make sense that body-based information for determining eye height follows the same principle. Because the variability in the visual estimates might be higher than that associated with the information about eye height from the body-based senses, body-based cues dominate visual ones in this case.

In summary, the research in this thesis demonstrates that there are cases in both, the real and virtual worlds where humans rely more on their body-based senses to inform their eye height. However, it is not clear yet of what exactly the body-based information consists. With the presented design of our experiments it is not possible to fully disentangle what I describe as body-based cues, which likely include but are not limited to proprioceptive, haptic and/or vestibular cues. Nevertheless, the empirical results presented in this dissertation imply that body-based cues are important (or even fundamental) for the perception of the spatial layout of our surrounding environment. Thus, VR might become even more important for investigating human perception, because of the offered flexibility and control it provides to manipulate different sensory information independently from each other. This might help to understand how humans combine different sources of information into a coherent percept of our surrounding environment.

7.2 Novel Practical / Applied Implications

The research presented in this dissertation demonstrates that eye height manipulations can be used to reduce or even counter the underestimation of perceived egocentric distances in IVEs. Interestingly, distance estimates are affected by manipulations of eye height regardless of whether a cognitive or action-based measure was used, suggesting that the effects are not due to a post-perceptual cognitive influence but occur due to a change in the scale of the perceived space. Furthermore, the effect of a manipulated eye height on perceived distances was visible immediately and I did not find any time related change in the distance estimates (e.g. that participants become more accurate over time) during the time course of the various conducted experiments (which lasted up to one hour spent in an IVE). Thus, eye height manipulations might be an effective and easy to implement tool to reduce distance underestimation in IVEs, which is usable in various applied scenarios.

Although the underestimation of distance can vary strongly between individuals (and also to some degree within individuals), a pretest to assess this individual underestimation can be done very quickly to determine the necessary eye height manipulation to reduce or counter this distance underestimation in IVEs. Thus, the user is enabled to improve his spatial performance regarding distances, and many applications like virtual prototyping, tele-operation and architectural design reviews will benefit from this improved accuracy. Furthermore, the results were similar regardless of the measures used, indicating that how the application is explored might not matter so much, for example in comparison to other approaches like minification. In addition, the empirical results in this thesis also demonstrate that it does not matter, whether the IVE is explored in a standing, sitting or even lying posture, as the perception of distance is constant as long as the head orientation is aligned with the gravity vector.

The results in this dissertation do not only provide evidence that eye height manipulations are a useful tool to reduce distance underestimation in IVEs. The presented results and hypotheses have also implications for many existing VR systems. Specifically, these results highlight the importance of a correct (or controlled) eye height calibration across different setups and systems, which is often either not easy to achieve or not feasible. Indeed, this can pose for example severe problems for multi-user setups, where multiple users explore and interact in one VE together. If it is not possible to guarantee a correct eye height for every user in such a scenario the virtual space will likely be perceived differently from every user, which hinders successful collaboration and interaction in such virtual spaces. Furthermore, consider for example a multi-projector large immersive screen setup using shutter glasses without head tracking: The necessary warping for screens, which are not planar, is usually calculated from a specific eye height. Thus, users which are larger or smaller than the rendered virtual eye height will underestimate or overestimate, respectively, compared to users which are matching closely the chosen eye height. With the provided perceptual theory in this thesis it is possible to quantify such effects to gain insight what perceptual distortions are due to the used screen setup and which distortions stem from the decoupling of the actual and virtual eye height.

In summary, the research presented in this dissertation implies that eye height manipulations are an effective tool to reduce or even counter distance underestimation in IVEs potentially across many different applications and also emphasizes the importance of the virtual eye height (calibration). This research also demonstrates why understanding and investigating human perception is important to understand the perception of IVEs in order to improve the utility of IVEs in general.

Chapter 8

Summary

In this dissertation, I have reviewed relevant literature in the field of visual perception in the real world and virtual worlds and literature from the field of computer science regarding technical aspects of IVEs. Furthermore, I reviewed literature indicating how eye height is important for perceiving our surrounding environment. Through the experiments presented in this thesis, I provide the first evidence that when the visual and body-based sources of information specifying eye height are in conflict, humans rely more on their body-based information to determine eye height for perceiving egocentric distances. These findings challenge traditional theories of perception, in which researchers have argued that the optical properties of the environment are sufficient to fully specify the spatial layout of an environment. In fact, the vast majority of perceptual psychologists still argues that only optical information is used by the visual system and that the process of transforming this information into a percept is isolated from influences from other senses [158]. In contrast to this view, I argue that our body-based senses can contribute important information to our perception of our surrounding environment. This is especially important for visual perception within VEs.

As virtual worlds are usually presented to an observer mainly using the visual modality, this finding is important for perceiving space within VEs, because as demonstrated with the experiments in this thesis, this does not mean that the observer is only relying on this presented information. Specifically, I provide evidence that this circumstance can be exploited by employing a virtual eye height manipulation to counter the commonly observed distance underestimation in head-mounted display virtual environments on an individual basis. Furthermore, the theory and accompanying experimental results in this dissertation cannot only be used to quantify the effect of a manipulated eye height in virtual reality, but also show that the relationship between body-based eye height and the angle of declination can be used to predictably alter an individuals' perceived egocentric distances in virtual reality to counter distance underestimation. Moreover, this approach has some advantages over other approaches that try to counter distance underestimation (i.e. it is easy to implement, it alters a limited set of visual cues), which might make it a useful tool to counter distance underestimation in diverse applications in various domains.

Bibliography

[1] N. Akkiraju, H. Edelsbrunner, P. Fu, and J. Qian. Viewing geometric protein structures from inside a CAVE. *Computer Graphics and Applications, IEEE*, 16(4):58–61, 1996. ISSN 0272-1716.

[2] A. Alaraj, M. G. Lemole, J. H. Finkle, R. Yudkowsky, A. Wallace, C. Luciano, P. P. Banerjee, S. H. Rizzi, and F. T. Charbel. Virtual reality training in neurosurgery: review of current status and future applications. *Surgical neurology international*, 2, 2011.

[3] L. Alberti. *On painting*. Penguin UK, 2005.

[4] I. V. Alexandrova, P. T. Teneva, de la Rosa, Stephan, U. Kloos, H. H. Bülthoff, and B. J. Mohler. Egocentric distance judgments in a large screen display immersive virtual environment. In *Proceedings of the 7th Symposium on Applied Perception in Graphics and Visualization*, pages 57–60, 2010.

[5] I. V. Alexandrova, M. Rall, M. Breidt, U. Kloos, G. Tullius, H. H. Bulthoff, and B. J. Mohler. Animations of Medical Training Scenarios in Immersive Virtual Environments. In *Digital Media and Digital Content Management (DMDCM), 2011 Workshop on*, pages 9–12, 2011.

[6] B. M. Altenhoff, P. E. Napieralski, L. O. Long, J. W. Bertrand, C. C. Pagano, S. V. Babu, and T. A. Davis. Effects of calibration to visual and haptic feedback on near-field depth perception in an immersive virtual environment. In *Proceedings of the ACM Symposium on Applied Perception*, pages 71–78, 2012.

[7] P. Backlund, H. Engstrom, C. Hammar, M. Johannesson, and M. Lebram. Sidh-a game based firefighter training simulation. In *Information Visualization, 2007. IV'07. 11th International Conference*, pages 899–907, 2007.

[8] J. N. Bailenson, J. Blascovich, A. C. Beall, and J. M. Loomis. Equilibrium theory revisited: Mutual gaze and personal space in virtual environments. *Presence: Teleoperators and Virtual Environments*, 10(6):583–598, 2001. ISSN 1054-7460.

[9] L. W. Barsalou. Grounded Cognition. *Annual REview of Psychology*, 59, 2008.

[10] A. C. Beall, J. M. Loomis, J. W. Philbeck, and T. G. Fikes. Absolute motion parallax weakly determines visual scale in real and virtual environments. In *Proceedings of the*

SPIE - The international Society for Optical Engineering, volume 2411, pages 288–297, 1995.

[11] G. Berkeley. *An essay towards a new theory of vision*. Aaron Rhames, 1709.

[12] G. P. Bingham and C. C. Pagano. The necessity of a perception–action approach to definite distance perception: Monocular distance perception to guide reaching. *Journal of Experimental Psychology: Human Perception and Performance*, 24(1):145, 1998. ISSN 0096-1523.

[13] G. P. Bingham, A. Bradley, M. Bailey, and R. Vinner. Accommodation, occlusion, and disparity matching are used to guide reaching: A comparison of actual versus virtual environments. *Journal of Experimental Psychology: Human Perception and Performance*, 27(6):1314, 2001. ISSN 0096-1523.

[14] F. Biocca. The Cyborg's Dilemma: Progressive Embodiment in Virtual Environments. *Journal of Computer-Mediated Communication*, 3(2), 1997.

[15] C. J. Bohil, B. Alicea, and F. A. Biocca. Virtual reality in neuroscience research and therapy. *Nature Reviews Neuroscience*, 12(12):752–762, 2011. ISSN 1471-003X.

[16] D. A. Bowman and R. P. McMahan. Virtual reality: how much immersion is enough? *Computer*, 40(7):36–43, 2007.

[17] P. Bradley. The history of simulation in medical education and possible future directions. *Medical education*, 40(3):254–262, 2006. ISSN 1365-2923.

[18] G. Bruder, A. Pusch, and F. Steinicke. Analyzing effects of geometric rendering parameters on size and distance estimation in on-axis stereographics. In *Proceedings of the ACM Symposium on Applied Perception*, pages 111–118, 2012.

[19] S. Bryson. Virtual reality in scientific visualization. *Communications of the ACM*, 39(5): 62–71, 1996. ISSN 0001-0782.

[20] S. Bryson. Virtual Reality: A Definition History-A Personal Essay. *arXiv preprint arXiv:1312.4322*, 2013.

[21] H. H. Buelthoff and A. L. Yuille. Shape-from-X: Psychophysics and computation. In *Fibers' 91, Boston, MA*, pages 235–246, 1991.

[22] J. L. Campos, P. Byrne, and H.-J. Sun. The brain weights body-based cues higher than vision when estimating walked distances. *European Journal of Neuroscience*, 31(10):1889–1898, 2010. ISSN 0953816X. doi: 10.1111/j.1460-9568.2010.07212.x.

[23] J. L. Campos, J. S. Butler, and H. H. Bülthoff. Multisensory integration in the estimation of walked distances. *Experimental Brain Research*, 218(4):551–565, 2012. ISSN 0014-4819. doi: 10.1007/s00221-012-3048-1.

[24] H. A. Carr. An introduction to space perception. 1935.

[25] W. Chen, J. Lu, and R. Nie, editors. *Design of Helicopter Training Simulator*, 2012. Atlantis Press. ISBN 9491216007.

[26] Y.-W. Chow. 3D Spatial Interaction with the Wii Remote for Head-Mounted Display Virtual Reality. *Proceedings of World Academy of Science: Engineering & Technology*, 50, 2009. ISSN 1307-6884.

[27] Y.-W. Chow. Low-Cost Multiple Degrees-of-Freedom Optical Tracking for 3D Interaction in Head-Mounted Display Virtual Reality. *International Journal of Network Security (2152-5064)*, 1(1), 2010. ISSN 2152-5064.

[28] A. Cioc, S. G. Djorgovski, C. Donalek, E. Lawler, F. Sauer, and G. Longo. Data Visualization Using Immersive Virtual Reality Tools. In *American Astronomical Society Meeting Abstracts*, volume 221, 2013.

[29] J. J. Clark and A. L. Yuille. *Data fusion for sensory information processing systems*. Kluwer Academic Publishers, 1990.

[30] E. M. Clerkin, M. W. Cody, J. K. Stefanucci, D. R. Proffitt, and B. A. Teachman. Imagery and fear influence height perception. *Journal of anxiety disorders*, 23(3):381–386, 2009.

[31] R. O. Coats, J. S. Pan, and G. P. Bingham. Perturbation of Perceptual Units Reveals Dominance Hierarchy in Cross Calibration. *Journal of experimental psychology. Human perception and performance*, 40(1):328–341, 2014.

[32] M. M. Cohen, S. M. Ebenholtz, and B. J. Linder. Effects of optical pitch on oculomotor control and the perception of target elevation. *Perception & psychophysics*, 57(4):433–440, 1995.

[33] E. Combe, J. Posselt, and A. Kemeny. 1: 1 Scale Perception in Virtual and Augmented Reality. In *18th International Conference on Artificial Reality and Telexistence*, pages 152–160, 2008.

[34] S. H. Creem-Regehr, P. Willemsen, A. A. Gooch, and W. B. Thompson. The Influence of Restricted Viewing Conditions on Egocentric Distance Perception: Implications for Real and Virtual Environments. *Perception*, 34(2):191–204, 2005.

[35] C. Cruz-Neira, D. J. Sandin, T. A. DeFanti, R. V. Kenyon, and J. C. Hart. The CAVE: audio visual experience automatic virtual environment. *Communications of the ACM*, 35 (6):64–72, 1992. ISSN 0001-0782.

[36] C. Cruz-Neira, D. J. Sandin, and T. A. DeFanti. Surround-screen projection-based virtual reality: the design and implementation of the CAVE. In *Proceedings of the 20th annual conference on Computer graphics and interactive techniques*, pages 135–142, 1993.

[37] J. E. Cutting. How the Eye Measures Reality and Virtual Reality. *Behavior Research Methods, Instruments, & Computers*, 29(1):27–36, 1997.

[38] J. E. Cutting and P. M. Vishton. Perceiving Layout and Knowing Distance: The Integration, Relative Potency and Contextual Use of Different Information about Depth. In W. Epstein and S. Rogers, editors, *Perception of Space and Motion*, pages 69–117. Academic Press, New York, 1995.

[39] M. D'Cruz, H. Patel, L. Lewis, S. Cobb, M. Bues, O. Stefani, T. Grobler, K. Helin, J. Viitaniemi, S. Aromaa, et al. Demonstration: VR-HYPERSPACE — The innovative use of virtual reality to increase comfort by changing the perception of self and space. In *Virtual Reality (VR), 2014 iEEE*, pages 167–168, 2014.

[40] M. Di Luca. New method to measure end-to-end delay of virtual reality. *Presence: Teleoperators and Virtual Environments*, 19(6):569–584, 2010. ISSN 1054-7460.

[41] M. W. Dixon, M. Wraga, D. R. Proffitt, and G. C. Williams. Eye Height Scaling of Absolute Size in Immersive and Nonimmersive Displays. *Journal of Experimental Psychology: Human Perception and Performance*, 26(2):582–593, 2000.

[42] T. J. Dodds, B. J. Mohler, and H. H. Bülthoff. Talk to the virtual hands: self-animated avatars improve communication in head-mounted display virtual environments. *PloS one*, 6(10):e25759, 2011. ISSN 1932-6203.

[43] D. Drascic and P. Milgram. Perceptual issues in augmented reality. In *Electronic Imaging: Science & Technology*, pages 123–134, 1996.

[44] P. S. Dunston, L. L. Arns, J. D. Mcglothlin, G. C. Lasker, and A. G. Kushner. An immersive virtual reality mock-up for design review of hospital patient rooms. In *Collaborative Design in Virtual Environments*, pages 167–176. Springer, 2011. ISBN 9400706049.

[45] F. H. Durgin, L. F. Fox, J. Lewis, and K. A. Walley. Perceptuomotor adaptation: More than meets the eye. *Psychonomic Society*, 7:103–104, 2002.

[46] F. H. Durgin, J. A. Baird, M. Greenburg, R. Russell, K. Shaughnessy, and S. Waymouth. Who is being deceived? The experimental demands of wearing a backpack. *Psychonomic Bulletin & Review*, 16(5):964–969, 2009.

[47] S. Egenfeldt-Nielsen, J. H. Smith, and S. P. Tosca. *Understanding video games: The essential introduction*. Routledge, 2013.

[48] W. Epstein, J. Park, and A. Casey. The current status of the size-distance hypotheses. *Psychological Bulletin*, 58(6):491, 1961. ISSN 1939-1455.

[49] M. O. Ernst and M. S. Banks. Humans integrate visual and haptic information in a statistically optimal fashion. *Nature*, 415(6870):429–433, 2002.

[50] C. S. Falcão and M. M. Soares. Ergonomics, Usability and Virtual Reality: A Review Applied to Consumer Product. *Advances in Usability Evaluation*, page 297, 2012. ISSN 1466560541.

[51] G. T. Fechner. *Elemente der Psychophysik, zweiter Teil.* Breitkopf & Härtel, 1860.

[52] G. T. Fechner. *Elemente der psychophysik*, volume 2. Breitkopf & Härtel, 1907.

[53] J. Fernández-Ruiz and R. D\'\iaz. Prism adaptation and aftereffect: specifying the properties of a procedural memory system. *Learning & Memory*, 6(1):47–53, 1999.

[54] C. Firestone. How "paternalistic" is spatial perception? Why wearing a heavy backpack doesn't—and couldn't—make hills look steeper. *Perspectives on Psychological Science*, 8 (4):455–473, 2013.

[55] J. M. Foley. Effect of distance information and range on two indices of visually perceived distance. *Perception*, 6(4):449–60, 1977.

[56] J. M. Foley. Binocular Distance Perception: Egocentric Distance Tasks. *Journal of Experimental Psychology: Human Perception and Performance*, 11(2):133–149, 1985.

[57] J. M. Foley and R. Field. Visually directed pointing as a function of target distance, direction, and available cues. *Perception & Psychophysics*, 12(3):263–268, 1972.

[58] J. Fox, J. N. Bailenson, and T. Ricciardi. Physiological responses to virtual selves and virtual others. *Journal of CyberTherapy & Rehabilitation*, 5(1):69–73, 2012.

[59] J. Frankenstein, B. J. Mohler, H. H. Bülthoff, and T. Meilinger. Is the map in our head oriented north? *Psychological Science*, 23(2):120–125, 2012. ISSN 0956-7976.

[60] G. Franz. *An empirical approach to the experience of architectural space.* Logos-Verlag, 2005.

[61] S. S. Fukusima, J. M. Loomis, and José A. Da Silva. Visual Perception of Egocentric Distance as Assessed by Triangulation. *Journal of Experimental Psychology: Human Perception and Performance*, 23(1):86–100, 1997.

[62] D. A. Gajewski, J. W. Philbeck, P. W. Wirtz, and D. Chichka. Angular declination and the dynamic perception of egocentric distance. *Journal of Experimental Psychology: Human Perception and Performance*, 40(1):361, 2014. ISSN 0096-1523.

[63] M. Geuss, J. Stefanucci, S. Creem-Regehr, and W. B. Thompson. Can I pass?: using affordances to measure perceived size in virtual environments. In *Proceedings of the 7th Symposium on Applied Perception in Graphics and Visualization*, pages 61–64, 2010.

[64] M. N. Geuss, J. K. Stefanucci, S. H. Creem-Regehr, and W. B. Thompson. Effect of viewing plane on perceived distances in real and virtual environments. *Journal of Experimental Psychology: Human Perception and Performance*, 38(5):1242, 2012. ISSN 0096-1523.

[65] J. J. Gibson. The Perception of Visual Surfaces. *American Journal of Psychology*, 63: 367–384, 1950.

[66] J. J. Gibson. The concept of affordances. *Perceiving, acting, and knowing*, pages 67–82, 1977.

[67] J. J. Gibson. *The ecological approach to visual perception*. Houghton, Mifflin and Company, Boston and MA and US, 1979. ISBN 0-39527-049-9.

[68] M. A. Gigante. Virtual reality: Enabling technologies, 1993.

[69] A. S. Gilinsky. Perceived Size and Distance in Visual Space. *Psychological Review*, 58: 460–482, 1951.

[70] E. B. Goldstein. *Sensation and perception*. Thomson Wadsworth, Belmont and Calif, 8 edition, 2010. ISBN 0495601497.

[71] T. Y. Grechkin, T. D. Nguyen, J. M. Plumert, J. F. Cremer, and J. K. Kearney. How does presentation method and measurement protocol affect distance estimation in real and virtual environments? *ACM Transactions on Applied Perception (TAP)*, 7(4):26, 2010. ISSN 1544-3558.

[72] P. Greenbaum. The lawnmower man. *Film and video*, 9(3):58–62, 1992.

[73] J. C. Hay and H. L. J. Pick. Visual and proprioceptive adaptation to optical displacement of the visual stimulus. *Journal of Experimental Psychology*, 71(1):150–158, 1966. doi: 10.1037/h0022611.

[74] Z. J. He, B. Wu, T. L. Ooi, G. Yarbrough, and J. Wu. Judging egocentric distance on the ground: Occlusion and surface integration. *PERCEPTION-LONDON-*, 33(7):789–806, 2004.

[75] R. Held. Plasticity in sensory-motor systems. *Scientific American*, 1965.

[76] D. Henry and T. Furness. Spatial Perception in Virtual Environments: Evaluating an Architectural Application. In *Virtual Reality Annual International Symposium*, pages 33–40. IEEE, 1993.

[77] D. M. Hoffman, A. R. Girshick, K. Akeley, and M. S. Banks. Vergence–accommodation conflicts hinder visual performance and cause visual fatigue. *Journal of vision*, 8(3):33, 2008.

[78] M. K. Holden. Virtual environments for motor rehabilitation: review. *Cyberpsychology & behavior*, 8(3):187–211, 2005. ISSN 1094-9313.

[79] E. B. Hsu, Y. Li, J. D. Bayram, D. Levinson, S. Yang, and C. Monahan. State of virtual reality based disaster preparedness and response training. *PLoS currents*, 5, 2013.

[80] J. J. Hutchison and J. M. Loomis. Does energy expenditure affect the perception of egocentric distance? A failure to replicate experiment 1 of Proffitt, Stefanucci, Banton, and Epstein (2003). *The Spanish journal of psychology*, 9(2):332–339, 2006.

[81] J. J. Hutchison and J. M. Loomis. Reply to Proffitt, Stefanucci, Banton, and Epstein. *The Spanish journal of psychology*, 9(02):343–345, 2006.

[82] V. Interrante, B. Ries, and L. Anderson. Distance perception in immersive virtual environments, revisited. In *Virtual Reality Conference, 2006*, pages 3–10, 2006.

[83] V. Interrante, B. Ries, J. Lindquist, M. Kaeding, and L. Anderson. Elucidating factors that can facilitate veridical spatial perception in immersive virtual environments. *Presence: Teleoperators and Virtual Environments*, 17(2):176–198, 2008. ISSN 1054-7460.

[84] J. A. Jones, E. A. Suma, D. M. Krum, and M. Bolas. Comparability of Narrow and Wide Field-of-view Head-mounted Displays for Medium-field Distance Judgments. In *Proceedings of the ACM Symposium on Applied Perception*, SAP '12, page 119, New York and NY and USA, 2012. ACM. ISBN 978-1-4503-1431-2. doi: 10.1145/2338676.2338701.

[85] F. Kellner, B. Bolte, G. Bruder, U. Rautenberg, F. Steinicke, M. Lappe, and R. Koch. Geometric calibration of head-mounted displays and its effects on distance estimation. *Visualization and Computer Graphics, IEEE Transactions on*, 18(4):589–596, 2012.

[86] R. V. Kenyon, D. Sandin, R. C. Smith, R. Pawlicki, and T. DeFanti. Size-Constancy in the CAVE. *Presence: Teleoperations and Virtual Environments*, 16(2):172–187, 2007.

[87] R. V. Kenyon, M. Phenany, D. Sandin, and T. DeFanti. Accommodation and size-constancy of virtual objects. *Annals of biomedical engineering*, 36(2):342–348, 2008.

[88] J. Ker, G. Hogg, N. Maran, and K. Walsh. Cost-effective simulation. *Cost effectiveness in medical education*, pages 61–71, 2010.

[89] F. P. Kilpatrick and W. H. Ittelson. The size-distance invariance hypothesis. *Psychological Review*, 60(4):223, 1953.

[90] E. Klein, J. E. Swan, G. S. Schmidt, M. A. Livingston, and O. G. Staadt. Measurement protocols for medium-field distance perception in large-screen immersive displays. In *Virtual Reality Conference, 2009. VR 2009. IEEE*, pages 107–113, 2009.

[91] J. M. Knapp. *The visual perception of egocentric distance in virtual environments*. PhD thesis, ProQuest Information & Learning, 2001.

[92] J. M. Knapp and J. M. Loomis. Limited Field of View of Head-Mounted Displays is not the Cause of Distance Underestimation in Virtual Environments. *Presence: Teleoperators and Virtual Environments*, 13(5):572–577, 2004. ISSN 1054-7460.

[93] M. Krijn, P. M. G. Emmelkamp, R. P. Olafsson, and R. Biemond. Virtual reality exposure therapy of anxiety disorders: A review. *Clinical psychology review*, 24(3):259–281, 2004. ISSN 0272-7358.

[94] M. W. Krueger. *Artificial reality II*, volume 10. Addison-Wesley Reading (Ma), 1991.

[95] M. Kubovy, W. Epstein, and S. Gepshtein. Foundations of visual perception. *Handbook of Psychology*, 2003.

[96] S. A. Kuhl. *The effects of geometric distortions on distance judgments in virtual environments*. PhD thesis, University of Utah, 2009.

[97] S. A. Kuhl, W. B. Thompson, and S. H. Creem-Regehr. Minification influences spatial judgments in virtual environments. In *Proceedings of the 3rd symposium on Applied perception in graphics and visualization*, pages 15–19. ACM, 2006. ISBN 1595934294.

[98] S. A. Kuhl, W. B. Thompson, and S. H. Creem-Regehr. HMD Calibration and Its Effects on Distance Judgments. *ACM Transactions on Applied Perception*, 6(3), 2009.

[99] A. Kulik, A. Kunert, S. Beck, R. Reichel, R. Blach, A. Zink, and B. Froehlich. C1x6: a stereoscopic six-user display for co-located collaboration in shared virtual environments. In *ACM Transactions on Graphics (TOG)*, volume 30, page 188, 2011.

[100] T. Kunnapas. DISTANCE PERCEPTION AS A FUNCTION OF AVAILABLE VISUAL CUES. *Journal of Experimental Psychology*, 77(4):523, 1968.

[101] B. R. Kunz, L. Wouters, D. Smith, W. B. Thompson, and S. H. Creem-Regehr. Revisiting the effect of quality of graphics on distance judgments in virtual environments: A comparison of verbal reports and blind walking. *Attention, Perception, & Psychophysics*, 71(6):1284–1293, 2009.

[102] M. S. Landy, L. T. Maloney, E. B. Johnston, and M. Young. Measurement and modeling of depth cue combination: In defense of weak fusion. *Vision Research*, 35(3):389–412, 1995.

[103] J. S. Lappin, A. L. Shelton, and J. J. Rieser. Environmental context influences visually perceived distance. *Perception & Psychophysics*, 68(4):571–581, 2006.

[104] K. Laver, S. George, S. Thomas, J. E. Deutsch, and M. Crotty. Virtual reality for stroke rehabilitation. *Stroke*, 43(2):e20–e21, 2012. ISSN 0039-2499.

[105] J. J. Laviola. Bringing VR and spatial 3D interaction to the masses through video games. *Computer Graphics and Applications, IEEE*, 28(5):10–15, 2008. ISSN 0272-1716.

[106] Le Corbusier. *Modulor 2: 1955 (la parole est aux usagers)*. Ed. de l'architecture d'aujourd'hui, 1955.

[107] D. N. Lee and H. Kalmus. The Optic Flow Field: The Foundation of Vision [and Discussion]. *Philosophical Transactions of the Royal Society B: Biological Sciences*, 290(1038): 169–179, 1980. ISSN 0962-8436. doi: 10.1098/rstb.1980.0089.

[108] A. I. Levine, S. DeMaria Jr, A. D. Schwartz, and A. J. Sim. *The Comprehensive Textbook of Healthcare Simulation*. Springer, 2013. ISBN 1461459931.

[109] M. Leyrer, S. A. Linkenauger, H. H. Bülthoff, U. Kloos, and B. Mohler. The influence of eye height and avatars on egocentric distance estimates in immersive virtual environments. In *Proceedings of the ACM SIGGRAPH Symposium on Applied Perception in Graphics and Visualization*, pages 67–74. ACM, 2011.

[110] Z. Li, J. Phillips, and F. Durgin. The underestimation of egocentric distance: evidence from frontal matching tasks. *Attention, Perception, & Psychophysics*, 73(7):2205–2217, 2011.

[111] Q. Lin, X. Xie, A. Erdemir, G. Narasimham, T. P. McNamara, J. Rieser, and B. Bodenheimer. Egocentric distance perception in real and HMD-based virtual environments: the effect of limited scanning method. In *Proceedings of the ACM SIGGRAPH Symposium on Applied Perception in Graphics and Visualization*, pages 75–82, 2011.

[112] E. A. Link. Combination Training Device for Student Aviators and Student Entertainment Apparatus. *US Patent Specification*, 127:82, 1930.

[113] J. M. Loomis and A. C. Beall. Visually Controlled Locomotion: Its Dependence on Optic Flow, Three-Dimensional Space Perception, and Cognition. *Ecological Psychology*, 10(3-4): 271–285, 1998.

[114] J. M. Loomis and J. Knapp. Visual Perception of Egocentric Distance in Real and Virtual Environments. In L. J. Hettinger and M. W. Haas, editors, *Virtual and Adaptive Environments*, pages 21–46. Erlbaum, Mahwah and NJ, 2003.

[115] J. M. Loomis and J. W. Philbeck. Measuring spatial perception with spatial updating and action. *Embodiment, ego-space, and action*, pages 1–43, 2008.

[116] J. M. Loomis, José A. Da Silva, N. Fujita, and S. S. Fukusima. Visual Space Perception and Visually Directed Action. *Journal of Experimental Psychology: Human Perception and Performance*, 18(4):906–921, 1992.

[117] J. M. Loomis, José A. Da Silva, J. W. Philbeck, and S. S. Fukusima. Visual Perception of Location and Distance. *Current Directions in Psychological Science*, 5(3), 1996.

[118] J. M. Loomis, J. J. Blascovich, and A. C. Beall. Immersive virtual environment technology as a basic research tool in psychology. *Behavior Research Methods, Instruments, & Computers*, 31(4):557–564, 1999.

[119] Loomis JM, Da Silva JA, Fujita N, and Fukusima SS. Visual space perception and visually directed action. *Journal of Experimental Psychology*, 18(4):906–921, 1992. ISSN 0096-1523.

[120] Z. Lozia. Driving Simulator–a supplementary tool in testing and training of drivers. *Speech at the Transbaltica*, pages 5–6, 2011.

[121] X. Luo, R. V. Kenyon, D. Kamper, D. Santin, and T. DeFanti. The Effects of Scene Complexity, Stereovision, and Motion Parallax on Size Constancy in a Mobile Virtual Environment. In *Proc.IEEE Virtual Reality*, pages 59–66, 2007.

[122] X. Luo, R. V. Kenyon, D. G. Kamper, D. J. Sandin, and T. A. DeFanti. On the determinants of size-constancy in a virtual environment. *The International Journal of Virtual Reality*, 8(1):43–51, 2009.

[123] L. S. Mark. Eyeheight-Scaled Information About Affordances: A Study of Sitting and Stair Climbing. *Journal of Experimental Psychology: Human Perception and Performance*, 13 (3):361–370, 1987.

[124] L. Matin and W. Li. Light and dark adaptation of visually perceived eye level controlled by visual pitch. *Perception & Psychophysics*, 57(1):84–104, 1995.

[125] T. Mazuryk and M. Gervautz. Virtual reality-history, applications, technology and future. *TU Vienna*, 1996.

[126] R. McCloy and R. Stone. Science, medicine, and the future: Virtual reality in surgery. *BMJ: British Medical Journal*, 323(7318):912, 2001.

[127] E. A. McManus, B. Bodenheimer, S. Streuber, de la Rosa, Stephan, H. H. Bülthoff, and B. J. Mohler. The influence of avatar (self and character) animations on distance estimation, object interaction and locomotion in immersive virtual environments. In *Proceedings of the ACM SIGGRAPH Symposium on Applied Perception in Graphics and Visualization*, pages 37–44, 2011.

[128] R. Messing and F. Durgin. Distance Perception and the Visual Horizon in Head-Mounted Displays. *ACM Transactions on Applied Perception*, 2(3):234–250, 2005.

[129] B. J. Mohler. *The Effect of Feedback Within a Virtual Environment on Human Distance Perception and Adaptation*. ProQuest. Dissertation University of Utah., 2007.

[130] B. J. Mohler, S. H. Creem-Regehr, and W. B. Thompson. The Influence of Feedback on Egocenteric Distance Judgments in Real and Virtual Environments. In *Proc. Symposium on Applied Perception in Graphics and Visualization*, pages 9–14, 2006.

[131] B. J. Mohler, W. B. Thompson, S. H. Creem-Regehr, P. Willemsen, Herbert L. Pick JR., and J. J. Rieser. Calibration of Locomotion Resulting from Visual Motion in a Treadmill-Based Virtual Environment. *ACM Transactions on Applied Perception*, 4(1), 2007.

[132] B. J. Mohler, H. H. Bülthoff, W. B. Thompson, and S. H. Creem-Regehr. A full-body avatar improves distance judgments in virtual environments. In *Proc. Symposium on Applied Perception in Graphics and Visualization*, 2008.

[133] B. J. Mohler, S. H. Creem-Regehr, W. B. Thompson, and H. H. Bülthoff. The Effect of Viewing a Self-Avatar on Distance Judgments in an HMD-Based Virtual Environment. *Presence: Teleoperators and Virtual Environments*, 19(3):230–242, 2010. ISSN 1054-7460. doi: 10.1162/pres.19.3.230.

[134] M. Mon-Williams and J. R. Tresilian. Some recent studies on the extraretinal contribution to distance perception. *PERCEPTION-LONDON-*, 28:167–182, 1999.

[135] M. Narayan, L. Waugh, X. Zhang, P. Bafna, and D. Bowman. Quantifying the benefits of immersion for collaboration in virtual environments. In *Proceedings of the ACM symposium on Virtual reality software and technology*, pages 78–81, 2005.

[136] V. R. Oculus. Oculus rift-virtual reality headset for 3d gaming. *URL: http://www.oculusvr.com*, 2012.

[137] T. L. Ooi, B. Wu, and Z. J. He. Distance Determination by the Angular Declination Below the Horizon. *Nature*, 414:197–200, 2001.

[138] J. Orlansky and J. String. Cost-effectiveness of flight simulators for military training. In *The Interservice/Industry Training, Simulation & Education Conference (I/ITSEC)*, volume 1. NTSA, 1979.

[139] J. S. Pan, R. O. Coats, and G. P. Bingham. Calibration is action specific but perturbation of perceptual units is not. *Journal of Experimental Psychology: Human Perception and Performance*, 40(1):404, 2014. ISSN 0096-1523.

[140] R. Pausch and T. Crea. A Literature Survey for Virtual Environments: Military Flight-Simulator Visual Systems and Simulator Sickness. Technical report, Charlottesville, VA, USA, 1992.

[141] L. J. Peters and G. R. Garinther. The effects of speech intelligibility on crew performance in an M1A1 tank simulator, 1990.

[142] J. W. Philbeck. *Processes underlying apparently paradoxical indications of extent.* PhD thesis, University of California, Santa Barbara, 1997.

[143] J. W. Philbeck and J. M. Loomis. Comparison of Two Indicators of Perceived Egocentric Distance Under Full-Cue and Reduced-Cue Conditions. *Journal of Experimental Psychology: Human Perception and Performance*, 23(1):72–85, 1997.

[144] L. Phillips, B. Ries, V. Interrante, M. Kaeding, and L. Anderson. Distance perception in npr immersive virtual environments, revisited. In *Proceedings of the 6th Symposium on Applied Perception in Graphics and Visualization*, pages 11–14, 2009.

[145] L. Phillips, B. Ries, M. Kaeding, and V. Interrante. Avatar self-embodiment enhances distance perception accuracy in non-photorealistic immersive virtual environments. In *Virtual Reality Conference (VR), 2010 IEEE*, pages 115–1148, 2010.

[146] I. V. Piryankova, de la Rosa, Stephan, U. Kloos, H. H. Bülthoff, and B. J. Mohler. Egocentric distance perception in large screen immersive displays. *Displays*, 34(2):153–164, 2013. ISSN 0141-9382.

[147] C. Pittman and LaViola Jr, Joseph J. Exploring head tracked head mounted displays for first person robot teleoperation. In *Proceedings of the 19th international conference on Intelligent User Interfaces*, pages 323–328, 2014.

[148] J. M. Plumert, J. K. Kearney, J. F. Cremer, and K. Recker. Distance perception in real and virtual environments. *ACM Transactions on Applied Perception (TAP)*, 2(3):216–233, 2005. ISSN 1544-3558.

[149] M. I. Posner, M. J. Nissen, and R. M. Klein. Visual dominance: an information-processing account of its origins and significance. *Psychological Review*, 83(2):157, 1976.

[150] D. R. Proffitt. Embodied Perception and the Economy of Action. *Perspectives on Psychological Science*, 1(2):110–122, 2006.

[151] D. R. Proffitt. Distance perception. *Current Directions in Psychological Science*, 15(3): 131–135, 2006.

[152] D. R. Proffitt. An action-specific approach to spatial perception. *Embodiment, ego-space, and action*, pages 179–202, 2008.

[153] D. R. Proffitt. An embodied approach to perception by what units are visual perceptions scaled? *Perspectives on Psychological Science*, 8(4):474–483, 2013.

[154] D. R. Proffitt and C. Caudek. Depth perception and the perception of events. *Handbook of Psychology*, 2002.

[155] D. R. Proffitt and S. A. Linkenauger. Perception viewed as a phenotypic expression. *Action science: Foundations of an emerging discipline*, pages 171–197, 2013.

[156] D. R. Proffitt, J. Stefanucci, T. Banton, and W. Epstein. The role of effort in perceiving distance. *Psychological Science*, 14(2):106–112, 2003. ISSN 0956-7976.

[157] D. R. Proffitt, J. Stefanucci, T. Banton, and W. Epstein. Reply to Hutchison and Loomis. *The Spanish journal of psychology*, 9(02):340–342, 2006.

[158] Z. Pylyshyn. Is vision continuous with cognition? The case for cognitive impenetrability of visual perception. *Behavioral and brain sciences*, 22(3):341–365, 1999. ISSN 1469-1825.

[159] K. M. Rand, M. R. Tarampi, S. H. Creem-Regehr, and W. B. Thompson. The importance of a visual horizon for distance judgments under severely degraded vision. *Perception*, 40: 143–154, 2011.

[160] R. S. Renner, B. M. Velichkovsky, and J. R. Helmert. The perception of egocentric distances in virtual environments-a review. *ACM Computing Surveys (CSUR)*, 46(2):23, 2013. ISSN 0360-0300.

[161] A. R. Richardson and D. Waller. The effect of feedback training on distance estimation in virtual environments. *Applied Cognitive Psychology*, 19(8):1089–1108, 2005.

[162] A. R. Richardson and D. Waller. Interaction with an immersive virtual environment corrects users' distance estimates. *Human Factors: The Journal of the Human Factors and Ergonomics Society*, 49(3):507–517, 2007. ISSN 0018-7208.

[163] B. E. Riecke, P. A. Behbahani, and C. D. Shaw. Display size does not affect egocentric distance perception of naturalistic stimuli. In *Proceedings of the 6th Symposium on Applied Perception in Graphics and Visualization*, pages 15–18, 2009.

[164] B. Ries, V. Interrante, M. Kaeding, and L. Anderson. The effect of self-embodiment on distance perception in immersive virtual environments. In *Proc.ACM Symposium on Virtual Reality Software and Technology*, pages 167–170, 2008.

[165] J. J. Rieser, D. H. Ashmead, C. R. Tayor, and G. A. Youngquist. Visual perception and the guidance of locomotion without vision to previously seen targets. *Perception*, 19:675–689, 1990.

[166] J. J. Rieser, J. H. L. Pick, D. H. Ashmead, and A. E. Garing. Calibration of Human Locomotion and Models of Perceptual-Motor Organization. *Journal of Experimental Psychology: Human Perception and Performance*, 21(3):480–497, 1995. ISSN 0096-1523.

[167] G. Riva. Virtual reality in psychotherapy: review. *Cyberpsychology & behavior*, 8(3): 220–230, 2005. ISSN 1094-9313.

[168] A. Rizzo and G. Kim. A SWOT analysis of the field of virtual reality rehabilitation and therapy. *Presence*, 14(2):119–146, 2005.

[169] A. Rizzo, T. D. Parsons, B. Lange, P. Kenny, J. G. Buckwalter, B. Rothbaum, J. Difede, J. Frazier, B. Newman, and J. Williams. Virtual reality goes to war: a brief review of the future of military behavioral healthcare. *Journal of clinical psychology in medical settings*, 18(2):176–187, 2011. ISSN 1068-9583.

[170] I. Rock and C. S. Harris. Vision and touch. *Scientific American*, 1967.

[171] I. Rock and J. Victor. Vision and touch: An experimentally created conflict between the two senses. *Science*, 143(3606):594–596, 1964.

[172] F. D. Rose, B. M. Brooks, and A. A. Rizzo. Virtual reality in brain damage rehabilitation: review. *Cyberpsychology & behavior*, 8(3):241–262, 2005. ISSN 1094-9313.

[173] K. Rosen. The history of simulation. In *The comprehensive textbook of healthcare simulation*, pages 5–49. Springer, 2013. ISBN 1461459923.

[174] L. B. Rosenberg. The effect of interocular distance upon operator performance using stereoscopic displays to perform virtual depth tasks. In *Virtual Reality Annual International Symposium, 1993., 1993 IEEE*, pages 27–32, 1993.

[175] C. S. Sahm, S. H. Creem-Regehr, W. B. Thompson, and P. Willemsen. Throwing Versus Walking as Indicators of Distance Perception in Real and Virtual Environments. *ACM Transactions on Applied Perception*, 1(3):35–45, 2005.

[176] L. Schmidt, J. Hegenberg, and L. Cramar. User studies on teleoperation of robots for plant inspection. *Industrial Robot: An International Journal*, 41(1):6–14, 2014.

[177] R. A. Schmidt and C. A. Wrisberg. Motor learning and performance. 2004.

[178] H. A. Sedgwick. *The visible horizon: A potential source of visual information for the perception of size and distance.* PhD thesis, ProQuest Information & Learning, US, 1973.

[179] H. A. Sedgwick. Section IV: Space and Motion Perception. In K. Boff, L. Kaufman, and J. Thomas, editors, *Handbook of Perception and Human Performance*, volume 1. Wiley-Interscience, New York, 1986.

[180] A. Seth, J. M. Vance, and J. H. Oliver. Virtual reality for assembly methods prototyping: a review. *Virtual reality*, 15(1):5–20, 2011. ISSN 1359-4338.

[181] F. Shao, A. J. Robotham, and K. Hon. Development of a 1:1 Scale True Perception Virtual Reality System for design review in automotive industry. 2012.

[182] M. J. Sinai, T. L. Ooi, and Z. J. He. Terrain influences the accurate judgement of distance. *Nature*, 395(6701):497–500, 1998. ISSN 00280836. doi: 10.1038/26747.

[183] M. Slater and M. Usoh. Body Centred Interaction in Immersive Virtual Environments. In N. M. Thalmann and D. Thalmann, editors, *Artificial Life and Virtual Reality*, pages 125–148. John Wiley and Sons, 1994.

[184] M. Slater and S. Wilbur. A framework for immersive virtual environments (FIVE): Speculations on the role of presence in virtual environments. *Presence: Teleoperators and Virtual Environments*, 6(6):603–616, 1997. ISSN 1054-7460.

[185] M. Slater, B. Spanlang, and D. Corominas. Simulating virtual environments within virtual environments as the basis for a psychophysics of presence. *ACM Transactions on Graphics (TOG)*, 29(4):92, 2010. ISSN 1450302106.

[186] M. Slater, B. Spanlang, M. V. Sanchez-Vives, and O. Blanke. First person experience of body transfer in virtual reality. *PloS one*, 5(5):e10564, 2010. ISSN 1932-6203.

[187] P. C. Smith and O. W. Smith. Ball throwing responses to photographically potrayed targets. *Journal of Experimental Psychology*, 62:223–233, 1961.

[188] R. Sousa, J. B. J. Smeets, and E. Brenner. Does size matter? *Perception*, 41(12):1532, 2012.

[189] J. K. Stefanucci and M. Geuss. Duck! Scaling the height of a horizontal barrier to body height. *Attention, Perception, & Psychophysics*, 72:1338–1349, 2010.

[190] J. K. Stefanucci and D. R. Proffitt. The roles of altitude and fear in the perception of height. *Journal of Experimental Psychology: Human Perception and Performance*, 35(2): 424, 2009. ISSN 0096-1523.

[191] J. K. Stefanucci and J. Storbeck. Don't look down: emotional arousal elevates height perception. *Journal of Experimental Psychology: General*, 138(1):131, 2009.

[192] F. Steinicke, G. Bruder, K. Hinrichs, M. Lappe, B. Ries, and V. Interrante. Transitional environments enhance distance perception in immersive virtual reality systems. In *Proceedings of the 6th Symposium on Applied Perception in Graphics and Visualization*, pages 19–26, 2009.

[193] F. Steinicke, G. Bruder, and S. Kuhl. Realistic perspective projections for virtual objects and environments. *ACM Transactions on Graphics (TOG)*, 30(5):112, 2011. ISSN 1450302106.

[194] J. Steuer. Defining virtual reality: Dimensions determining telepresence. *Journal of communication*, 42(4):73–93, 1992. ISSN 1460-2466.

[195] A. E. Stoper and M. M. Cohen. Judgments of eye level in light and in darkness. *Perception & Psychophysics*, 40(5):311–316, 1986.

[196] A. E. Stoper and M. M. Cohen. Effect of structured visual environments on apparent eye level. *Perception & Psychophysics*, 46(5):469–475, 1989.

[197] G. M. Stratton. Vision without inversion of the retinal image. *Psychological Review*, 4(4): 341, 1897.

[198] R. T. Surdick, E. T. Davis, R. A. King, and L. F. Hodges. The perception of distance in simulated visual displays — A comparison of the effectiveness and accuracy of multiple depth cues across viewing distances. *Presence: Teleoperators and Virtual Environments*, 6(5):513–531, 1997. ISSN 1054-7460.

[199] I. E. Sutherland. The ultimate display. *Multimedia: From Wagner to virtual reality*, 1965.

[200] M. J. Tarr and W. H. Warren. Virtual reality in behavioral neuroscience and beyond. *Nature Neuroscience*, 5:1089–1092, 2002.

[201] W. Thompson, R. Fleming, S. Creem-Regehr, and J. K. Stefanucci. *Visual perception from a computer graphics perspective*. CRC Press, 2011.

[202] W. B. Thompson, P. Willemsen, A. A. Gooch, S. H. Creem-Regehr, J. M. Loomis, and A. C. Beall. Does the Quality of the Computer Graphics Matter When Judging Distances in Visually Immersive Environments? *Presence: Teleoperators and Virtual Environments*, 13(5):560–571, 2004. ISSN 1054-7460.

[203] M. Wagner. *The geometries of visual space*. Psychology Press, 2006.

[204] J. Walker, R. Zhang, and S. A. Kuhl. Minification and gap affordances in head-mounted displays. In *Proceedings of the ACM Symposium on Applied Perception*, page 124, 2012.

[205] D. Waller and A. R. Richardson. Correcting distance estimates by interacting with immersive virtual environments: Effects of task and available sensory information. *Journal of Experimental Psychology: Applied*, 14(1):61–72, 2008.

[206] D. Waller, J. M. Loomis, and D. B. M. Haun. Body-based senses enhance knowledge of directions in large-scale environments. *Psychonomic Bulletin & Review*, 11(1):157–163, 2004.

[207] C. Ware, C. Gobrecht, and M. Paton. Algorithm for dynamic disparity adjustment. In *IS&T/SPIE's Symposium on Electronic Imaging: Science & Technology*, pages 150–156, 1995.

[208] J. W. H. Warren and S. Whang. Visual Guidance of Walking Through Apertures: Body Scaled Information for Affordances. *Journal of Experimental Psychology: Human Perception and Performance*, 13:371–383, 1987.

[209] W. H. Warren. Perceiving affordances: Visual guidance of stair climbing. *Journal of Experimental Psychology: Human Perception and Performance*, 10(5):683–703, 1984. ISSN 0096-1523. doi: 10.1037/0096-1523.10.5.683.

[210] Z. Wartell, L. F. Hodges, and W. Ribarsky. Balancing fusion, image depth and distortion in stereoscopic head-tracked displays. In *Proceedings of the 26th annual conference on Computer graphics and interactive techniques*, pages 351–358, 1999.

[211] B. A. Watson and L. F. Hodges. Using texture maps to correct for optical distortion in head-mounted displays. In *Virtual Reality Annual International Symposium, 1995. Proceedings*, pages 172–178, 1995.

[212] P. Willemsen and A. A. Gooch. Perceived egocentric distances in real, image-based, and traditional virtual environments. In *Virtual Reality, 2002. Proceedings. IEEE*, pages 275–276, 2002.

[213] P. Willemsen, M. B. Colton, S. H. Creem-Regehr, and W. B. Thompson. The effects of head-mounted display mechanics on distance judgments in virtual environments. In *Proceedings of the 1st Symposium on Applied perception in graphics and visualization*, pages 35–38, 2004.

[214] P. Willemsen, A. A. Gooch, W. B. Thompson, and S. H. Creem-Regehr. Effects of Stereo Viewing Conditions on Distance Perception in Virtual Environments. *Presence: Teleoperators and Virtual Environments*, 17(1):91–101, 2008. ISSN 1054-7460.

[215] P. Willemsen, M. B. Colton, S. H. Creem-Regehr, and W. B. Thompson. The effects of head-mounted display mechanical properties and field of view on distance judgments in virtual environments. *ACM Transactions on Applied Perception (TAP)*, 6(2):8, 2009. ISSN 1544-3558.

[216] B. Williams, T. Rasor, and G. Narasimham. Distance perception in virtual environments: a closer look at the horizon and the error. In *Proceedings of the 6th Symposium on Applied Perception in Graphics and Visualization*, pages 7–10. ACM, 2009.

[217] M. Wilson. Six views of embodied cognition. *Psychonomic Bulletin & Review*, 9(4): 625–636, 2002.

[218] B. G. Witmer and W. J. Sadowski. Nonvisually guided locomotion to a previously viewed target in real and virtual environments. *Human Factors: The Journal of the Human Factors and Ergonomics Society*, 40(3):478–488, 1998. ISSN 0018-7208.

[219] J. K. Witt, D. R. Proffitt, and W. Epstein. Perceiving distance: A role of effort and intent. *PERCEPTION-LONDON-*, 33:577–590, 2004.

[220] J. K. Witt, J. K. Stefanucci, C. R. Riener, and D. R. Proffitt. Seeing beyond the target: Environmental context affects distance perception. *PERCEPTION-LONDON-*, 36(12): 1752, 2007.

[221] A. J. Woods, T. Docherty, and R. Koch. Image distortions in stereoscopic video systems. In *IS&T/SPIE's Symposium on Electronic Imaging: Science and Technology*, pages 36–48, 1993.

[222] A. J. Woods, J. W. Philbeck, and J. V. Danoff. The various perceptions of distance: an alternative view of how effort affects distance judgments. *Journal of Experimental Psychology: Human Perception and Performance*, 35(4):1104, 2009. ISSN 0096-1523.

[223] R. S. Woodworth and H. Schlosberg. *Experimental psychology*. Oxford and IBH Publishing, 1954.

[224] M. Wraga. The role of eye height in perceiving affordances and object dimensions. *Perception & Psychophysics*, 61(3):490–507, 1999.

[225] M. Wraga. Using Eye Height in Different Postures to Scale the Heights of Objects. *Journal of Experimental Psychology: Human Perception and Performance*, 25(2):518–530, 1999.

[226] M. Wraga and D. R. Proffitt. Mapping the zone of eye-height utility for seated and standing observers. *Perception*, 29:1361–1383, 2000.

[227] B. Wu, T. L. Ooi, and Z. J. He. Perceiving Distance Accurately by a Directional Process of Integrating Ground Information. *Nature*, 428:73–77, 2004.

[228] J. Wu, Z. J. He, and T. L. Ooi. Visually perceived eye level and horizontal midline of the body trunk influenced by optic flow. *Perception*, 34(9):1045–1060, 2005. ISSN 0301-0066. doi: 10.1068/p5416.

[229] N. Yee, J. N. Bailenson, and N. Ducheneaut. The Proteus effect implications of transformed digital self-representation on online and offline behavior. *Communication Research*, 36(2): 285–312, 2009. ISSN 0093-6502.

[230] R. Zhang, A. Nordman, J. Walker, and S. A. Kuhl. Minification affects verbal-and action-based distance judgments differently in head-mounted displays. *ACM Transactions on Applied Perception (TAP)*, 9(3):14, 2012. ISSN 1544-3558.